INTENTION AND ACHIEVEMENT

INTENTION
AND
ACHIEVEMENT

AN ESSAY ON THE NOVELS
OF FRANÇOIS MAURIAC

BY

J. E. FLOWER
Lecturer in French
University of East Anglia

CLARENDON PRESS · OXFORD
1969

Oxford University Press, Ely House, London W.1

GLASGOW NEW YORK TORONTO MELBOURNE WELLINGTON
CAPE TOWN SALISBURY IBADAN NAIROBI LUSAKA ADDIS ABABA
BOMBAY CALCUTTA MADRAS KARACHI LAHORE DACCA
KUALA LUMPUR SINGAPORE HONG KONG TOKYO

PRINTED IN GREAT BRITAIN
BY THE CAMELOT PRESS LTD.
LONDON AND SOUTHAMPTON

FOR
ANDREW, CHRISTOPHER, AND STEPHEN

ACKNOWLEDGEMENTS

A NY book which emerges even only partially from a
thesis, inevitably owes much to those who have helped
it along its way. This one is no exception, and it is with
pleasure that I am able to acknowledge my debts to a number of
people in particular: my supervisor Professor George Lehmann
for his friendly and constant encouragement, and his keen insight
which enabled me to avoid many a pitfall; Professor R. J. North
for his knowledgeable criticisms and observations on this and
other work in connection with Mauriac; Professor H. T. Mason
for having read and commented on several chapters of the
original thesis; and Monsieur François Mauriac who has always
been willing to discuss his work in letters or interviews. In addition
I should like to thank the University Library Staff at Reading and
in particular the Inter-Library Loans Department; Monsieur
François Chapon and Mademoiselle Jacqueline Zacchi of the
Fonds Doucet in Paris who have been most friendly and helpful
at all times; Macmillan & Co. Ltd., and the Editors of *French
Studies* for their kind permission in allowing me to reproduce in
slightly different form material which has already appeared
elsewhere; and the Clarendon Press for their consideration and
splendid efficiency at all stages. Above all, however, my greatest
debt must go to my wife who has suffered the moodiness and
short temper induced by this work with soothing good sense
and patience.

   To others who are too numerous to mention here, staff,
students, and friends alike, my thanks and assurance that all
unacknowledged peculiarities and errors are entirely my own.

J. E. F.

Reading, November, 1968

CONTENTS

•

Acknowledgement: Frontispiece—photograph by Jean-Marie Marcel, Paris.

ABBREVIATIONS

IN the interest of general tidiness in the footnotes I have employed the abbreviations listed below. Where texts other than those contained in the *Œuvres complètes* edition of Mauriac's work have been quoted, the reference is given in brackets. All other relevant bibliographical details are to be found in the *Select Bibliography* on page 116.

A   *L'Agneau* (Flammarion, 1954)

AA   *Un Adolescent d'autre fois*, (Flammarion, 1969)

AN   *Les Anges noirs* (Livre de poche)

B   *Bordeaux*

BD   *Le Baillon dénoué*

BL   *Le Baiser au lépreux*

B-N   *Bloc-notes*

CP   *Ce qui était perdu*

CQJC   *Ce que je crois*

CS   *La Chair et le sang*

D   *Destins*

DA   *Le Désert de l'amour* (Livre de poche)

DM   *Dieu et Mammon*

ECC   *L'Enfant chargé de chaînes*

EF   *L'Education des filles* (Corrêa, 1933)

FF   *Le Fleuve de feu*

FH   *Le Fils de l'homme*

FN   *La Fin de la nuit* (Grasset, 1935)

G   *Génitrix*

GAL   *Galigaï* (J'ai lu)

J   *Journal* (Volumes II and III Grasset, 1937 and 1940; IV and V Flammarion, 1950 and 1953)

JTA   *Journal d'un homme de trente ans*

LO   *Lettres ouvertes* (Editions du Rocher, 1952)

M   *Le Mal* (Grasset, 1935)

MF	*Le Mystère Frontenac* (Livre de poche)
MI	*Mémoires intérieurs*
MP	*Mémoires politiques*
NB-N	*Le Nouveau Bloc-notes*
NMI	*Nouveaux Mémoires intérieurs*
NV	*Le Nœud de vipères* (Livre de poche)
P	*Préséances*
PA	*La Pierre d'achoppement* (Editions du Rocher, 1951)
PC	*Paroles catholiques* (Plon, 1954)
PH	*La Pharisienne*
PL	*Plongées*
PR	*La Province*
PV	*Le Pain vivant* (Flammarion, 1955)
R	*Le Roman*
RB	*La Rencontre avec Barrès*
RP	*La Robe prétexte*
RSP	*Le Romancier et ses personnages*
S	*Le Sagouin* (Editions de la Palantine, 1951)
SBC	*Souffrance et bonheur du chrétien*
TD	*Thérèse Desqueyroux* (Livre de poche)
VMP	*La Vie et la mort d'un poète*
O.C.	*Œuvres complètes*

L'auteur dans son œuvre, doit être comme Dieu dans l'Univers, présent partout, et visible nulle part.

GUSTAVE FLAUBERT

Le roman catholique ce n'est pas celui qui ne nous entretient que de bons sentiments, c'est celui où la vie de la foi s'affronte avec les passions. Il faut rendre le plus sensible possible le tragique mystère du salut [...] l'expérience vécue de l'amour divin n'est pas du domaine du roman.

GEORGES BERNANOS

INTRODUCTION

THE last of five children, Mauriac was born at Bordeaux on 11 October 1885. His father died from a tumour on the brain two years later in June, and the children were brought up by their mother, with considerable assistance from her brother-in-law Louis. After the father's death Mme Mauriac and her children lodged with the maternal grandmother in the rue Duffour-du-Bergier, the first of a number of moves taking them in turn to the rue Vital Carles in 1894, to the corner of the rue Margaux and the rue de Cheverus in 1899 and eventually to the rue Rolland where Mme Mauriac had bought a house. During these years Mauriac's early education before attending the Lycée de Bordeaux and eventually the University was solidly Catholic, and this together with his weak physique and timid nature all helped to make him an introspective young man who, in spite of his undoubted intellectual ability and insatiable appetite for reading, gave little indication of the public role he was to play in subsequent years. The temporary attraction of Marc Sangnier's Social Catholic movement *Le Sillon* traced in *L'Enfant chargé de chaînes*,[1] and his move to Paris to study at the Ecole de Chartes provided him with an opportunity to break out of the enclosed family life he knew at Bordeaux and devote himself to literature. Mauriac soon became involved with various reviews, and one of these, *La Revue du Temps présent*, directed by Charles Francis Caillard, published his first volume of poems *Les Mains jointes* which was encouragingly reviewed in 1910 by Maurice Barrès. More significantly perhaps for the development later in his life of his interest in social and political matters, was his participation first in the *Amitié de France* which appeared in 1907 and five years later in the

[1] See below, pp. 32–42.

supplementary periodical *Les Cahiers de l'Amitié de France*.[1]

The first number of the *Cahiers* summarizes the aims of the whole project: 'Les buts religieux, catholiques, artistiques, sociaux, sont de part et d'autre identiques.'[2] All contributions to the review are based firmly on the Catholic faith: 'on ne trouvera jamais dans *L'Amitié de France* rien qui aille le moins du monde à l'encontre de la doctrine catholique'.[3] Only through Catholicism could the decadence spreading through the field of art and literature be effectively fought,[4] and Georges Dumesnil, who gave his patronage and occasionally his pen to these reviews, makes the same point in 1912 in a survey of several works by Catholic authors which, he argues, owe their greatness not to their apology for Catholicism but because Catholicism infuses their every aspect.[5] Such writing on literary matters appears side by side with political commentaries and religious exegeses, and in 1910 the *Amitié de France* proudly quotes a letter from the Pope, Pius X, encouraging them in their efforts to act as guides for the adolescent generation.

Mauriac's name does not appear at the foot of articles as frequently as those of his young associates, though from 1913 he and Valéry-Radot were given the task of reviewing books and plays. His participation in administrative duties and his friendship for his colleagues (in particular André Lafon) indicate well enough, however, that Mauriac shared their sympathies, though to what degree it is of course impossible to say.

Marriage in 1913 to Mlle Jeanne Lafont, the daughter of an influential and high-ranking bank official, and the years of the First World War did nothing to stem Mauriac's increasing literary output, and by 1921 a further three novels and an additional volume of verse had appeared. During the next fifteen years Mauriac devoted himself almost exclusively to literature, his achievements highlighted by the Grand Prix du Roman awarded for *Le Désert de l'amour*, and by the classification of *Thérèse Desqueyroux* as one of the dozen best French novels in the

---

[1] The development and influence of these groups has been extensively examined by the abbé Maugendre in *La Renaissance catholique*, Paris, 1963, Vol. 1.

[2] June 1912.   [3] *Amitié de France*, February–April 1907, p. 3.

[4] Ibid., 1908, p. 4.   [5] Ibid., 1912, p. 210.

first half of the century by a 'jury' of eminent literary figures including Colette, Henri Mondor and Jean Paulhan. It was also during this period that Mauriac experienced the crisis in his life that considerably influenced his career as an imaginative writer and which he explores in *Souffrances et bonheur du chrétien*. As Dr. Cecil Jenkins has recently indicated, however, at no time did Mauriac lose his faith, but the effect which this experience had on his life and work can none the less be conveniently referred to as a 'conversion'. The thirties saw a new Catholic vitality in his writing, but this was short lived and Mauriac turned more readily to journalism and Catholic essay writing, with his *Vie de Jésus* in particular arousing considerable hostility for its direct, human portrayal of Christ. The real turning point was marked by the advent of the Spanish Civil War: 'J'ai commencé à me détacher de la fiction au moment de la guerre d'Espagne, par exemple. Je vivais jusque-là dans une espèce de rêve, de monde fictif [. . .].'[1] Mauriac's private convictions were now irrevocably involved in a matter of public, world-wide dispute: 'La guerre d'Espagne . . . Je l'aurais vécue à une profondeur que je suis seul à pouvoir mesurer. Tout le drame du catholicisme s'y trouvait impliqué.'[2] Together with Jacques Maritain and a minority group of Catholics, Mauriac fought to dissociate the Catholic Church from a fatal compromise with fascist aggression. Mauriac was committed, yet the extent of his commitment was always to be determined by his faith: 'Que la passion politique m'entraîne ou m'égare, il n'en reste pas moins que je suis engagé dans ces problèmes d'en-bas, pour des raisons d'en-haut.'[3] This refusal of unquestioning political commitment has resulted on many occasions in charges of hypocrisy, but Mauriac is aware of the consequences and takes some pride in his ability to remain detached: 'il existe une fidélité dont je tire quelque gloire, celle qui m'a toujours rendu impropre à subir les directives d'un parti, et qui même dans l'Eglise (que de toute mon âme je souhaite servir, que je crois avoir, à ma manière, bien servie), m'a empêché de figurer parmi les serviteurs commodes: cette fidélité qui naît du scrupule de ne rien écrire que je ne pense vraiment'.[4] In the more

[1] M. Chapsal, *Les Ecrivains en personne*, Paris, 1960, p. 136.
[2] *NMI*, p. 118. [3] *B-N*, p. 69. [4] *LO*, p. 53.

recent years of the Fifth Republic his outspoken allegiance for de Gaulle has been born of this same need to be free: 'comme je n'ai jamais été inféodé à aucun parti, j'ai toujours obéi en toutes circonstances à mon instinct, et jamais à les impératifs et à des directives, comme un socialiste ou un communiste. C'est sur ce plan-là, d'ailleurs, que je ressemble le plus à de Gaulle. Nous sommes l'un et l'autre, de tous les Français engagés, les moins gênés aux entournures, et réellement les plus libres.'[1]

In 1952 Mauriac was awarded the Nobel Prize for literature, and it is for his vast body of writing and especially his novels that he will be remembered by future generations, for it is in this work that the real Mauriac is to be found. One of his favourite recurring themes is that of the mask, the assumed persona hiding the true self which can only be discovered through analysis, decomposition, or confession. Beyond Mauriac's role as a political observer lies the man whose novels trace the spiritual crisis of his own life and that of society around him. But Mauriac's task is not only to be illustrative, he must also convince; and that without becoming didactic. Throughout this immensely varied and productive period, the faith which has dictated his political affiliations, the 'roc immuable' of which he speaks in Le Romancier et ses personnages, remains constant, and together with his task for the moody landscape of his native bordelais region forms the basis on which all his novels are built.

These are the basic but essential facts about Mauriac's life, recounted by the majority of his critics[2] and most interestingly of all by Mauriac himself in the Postface to Nouveaux Mémoires intérieurs and the Préface to Mémoires politiques. By now Mauriac has become one of the most scrutinized writers in France of this century, claiming the attention of more than thirty full-length studies and several thousand articles. The longest to date and with little doubt the most enthusiastic remains Mme Nelly Cormeau's L'Art de François Mauriac,[3] but in spite of her copious illustration and impassioned defence of Mauriac in the face of Sartre's

---

[1] NMI, p. 243.

[2] See in particular the books by Jenkins, North, and Rideau.

[3] Details of this and other works mentioned here are to be found in the Bibliography.

criticism the work lacks any real direction. Equally sympathetic general studies are to be found in the books by Alain Palante, *Mauriac, le roman et la vie*, Emile Rideau, *Comment lire François Mauriac*, Joseph Majault, *Mauriac et l'art du roman*, and the more recent *Mauriac par lui-même* by Pierre-Henri Simon. Professor North's *Le Catholicisme dans l'œuvre de François Mauriac* remains the only study to date devoted to this particular aspect of Mauriac's work. There are also several books in English: the short general studies by Martin Jarrett-Kerr and Cecil Jenkins *François Mauriac* and *Mauriac*; the brilliantly incisive essay in Conor Cruise O'Brien's volume *Maria Cross*; Michael Moloney's study, interesting above all for its chapters on influences and style, and Professor Stratford's absorbing comparative work on Mauriac and Graham Greene. Hostile criticism is found particularly in Jacques Vier's *François Mauriac, romancier catholique?* and in Pol Vandromme's *La Politique littéraire de François Mauriac*.

With the exception of one of his earliest critics Charles du Bos and more recently Professor Stratford, and in spite of the apparent content of a number of critical studies, no commentators have paid adequate attention to the basic problem of the Catholic novel and to Mauriac's consideration of it. It has, to be sure, been acknowledged as a distinctive form but only in as much as it is a piece of writing which bears witness in some way to the Catholic faith. In other words it is a form of committed literature, but beyond this little attention has been given to the limiting effects of this commitment nor has the basic problem of incorporating a personal belief in a piece of imaginative literature in such a way that it does not obtrude been adequately examined. Sartre in his article 'Monsieur François Mauriac et la liberté' in which he accuses Mauriac of oversimplification and of manipulating his characters, certainly has some pertinent remarks to make, though, as Professor Stratford has pointed out, Mauriac was well aware of these difficulties and has not infrequently admitted that *La Fin de la nuit*, the target for Sartre's attack, is not one of his better novels. Professor Albert Sonnenfeld in an article 'The Catholic novelist and the Supernatural'[1] has indicated some of the characteristic features of this type of writing: the clumsy direct intervention of

[1] *French Studies*, October 1968, pp. 307–19.

God's will through miraculous events or abrupt, unprepared conversions; the intervention by the author to point a moral or direct his reader's attention; the private unsolicited confession by letter or journal; the appeal made to an undefined deity or omniscient power; the more subtle use of allusion and symbol. Of these Mauriac's novels offer us many interesting examples. But it is not on account of such detail as this that the Catholic novel should be considered a distinct type in its own right, indeed many of these features are to be found in literature which is in no way Catholic in inspiration. Moreover even within the relatively narrow context of French literature the term 'Catholic novel' is one to be used with some latitude and uncertainty. Indeed if we take for example Bernanos' *Sous le soleil de Satan*, a melodramatic, highly coloured clash between the forces of good and evil; Julien Green's *Moïra*, the account of the extreme effects of Protestantism on an American student; Cesbron's *Les Saints vont en enfer* which deals with the problem of the worker priests and in some ways is little more than an elaborate form of semi-documentary writing, and *Le Nœud de vipères*, the intricate account of a personal recantation, we at once have four novels all of which have been labelled Catholic but which in style and form are quite different. The problem is clearly a large one and as far as Mauriac is concerned only Du Bos and Stratford have made any satisfactory attempts to solve it, but again each approach is limited. Du Bos' essay on the Catholic novel admits the essential problem of combining the 'éléments impurs' of human life and the revealed truth of the Catholic faith, but his *personal* acceptance of that faith at once places him in a position which will not necessarily be shared by all his fellow critics. His conviction that a Catholic has a greater understanding of life and therefore an advantage over the atheist novelist will clearly not be acceptable to all. Professor Stratford also admits the basic problem[1] and goes some way to analysing Mauriac's discussion of it, but he only really considers Mauriac's self-confessed Catholic novels as evidence for any claim that it may have been solved.

Mauriac's aims and intention as a novelist during some forty years of writing have been to exemplify to others his own firm

[1] P. Stratford, *Faith and Fiction*, Indiana, 1963, p. 201.

conviction that mankind is assured of God's love: 'nous sommes aimés. Voilà le fond de tout.'[1] 'Il nous dit Lui-même que le Fils de l'Homme est venu chercher et sauver ce qui était perdu, oui, *tout* ce qui était perdu, et non pas seulement tel ou tel à qui il aurait consacré en particulier une avare goutte de sang.'[2] Yet against this stands his description of a particular segment of bourgeois society with its families decaying and doomed to extinction. This is the problem stated in its simplest terms and one of which Mauriac becomes increasingly aware in the course of his career. Implied values are not sufficient, particularly for the demanding Catholic critic, yet as a novelist Mauriac is very aware of the danger of didactic literature. His attempts to incorporate his personal faith in the public statements that are his novels are various: the semi-autobiographical account of his relationship with Social Catholicism as a young man, the harsh castigation of the attitude of mind which raises material values over spiritual ones, the idealized portrait of a family in *Le Mystère Frontenac*, or the allegory of Christ's passion in *L'Agneau*. Too frequently, however, such attempts are doomed to fail and Mauriac is open to the accusation of having implanted a particular point of view and in consequence of having falsified his picture of society. In order to avoid the charge of didacticism or of manipulation, therefore, the Catholic element of the novel must be included in such a way that it is an essential part of the structure of the book which without it would crumble. As we shall see Mauriac succeeds by allowing a pagan natural cycle of events to carry a Christian message. It is not enough to argue that *Le Nœud de vipères* and *Les Anges noirs* are Catholic simply because they are 'fondés sur la Révélation';[3] what is essential is to ascertain how Mauriac has worked the forces of Grace into the novels in such a way that they have become an integral part of them. In this way for the critic who from the outset denies the value of the Catholic faith Mauriac's intention may remain unacceptable, but his achievement will none the less deserve acknowledgement.

In this essay I have, as far as possible, attempted to avoid what has been said about Mauriac and his work before, particularly where I find myself in agreement. Some overlap is unavoidable

[1] *LO*, p. 117.   [2] *FH*, p. 190.   [3] O.C. III. ii.

of course, particularly in Chapter Three, Mauriac's Bourgeois World, but even here I have tried to emphasize the narrow inbred nature of Mauriac's society and his implication that it is doomed to extinction: physical decay is as important as spiritual aridity. Elsewhere I have examined those areas where Mauriac has either been experimenting (Chapter Two) or where he has deliberately set out to correct what many have found to be too pessimistic a view of humanity. In this way I feel that *Le Mystère Frontenac* with its emphasis on the *sacred* nature of the family may be considered a Catholic novel.

I have for the most part used the term 'Catholic novel' though there are occasions when 'religious' or 'Christian novel' would have been just as appropriate. If I have caused offence I apologize: I am not a Catholic myself but I do feel that the general values represented by Christianity are frequently as important to Mauriac as any specific Catholic interpretation. No doubt there are points which do belong to the latter category and which I have missed. My main concern, however, has been an attempt to illustrate how Mauriac has sought to incorporate his private conviction of the reality of God's Grace and of Divine love in the public vehicle of his novels, and how in some cases he has succeeded. With this in mind the first chapter outlines Mauriac's personal religious crisis and his theories of novel writing.

I

THE INTENTION:
CATHOLICISM AND THE NOVEL

Ce n'est pas un changement qui s'est fait en moi, c'est moins encore une
révolution. Mais tout simplement, j'ai commencé d'y voir plus clair.
GEORGES BERNANOS
Un romancier soumis à Dieu, lui soumet le monde dans ses livres.
FRANÇOIS MAURIAC

UNLIKE many leading French Catholic intellectuals in the
twentieth century Mauriac's faith did not come to him
through a sudden conversion or revelation: 'Il ne s'est
jamais rien passé dans ma vie que j'aie pu interpréter comme un
appel.'[1] Faith came to the young Mauriac as part of his family
inheritance, something which, as he confesses in *Dieu et Mammon*
and *Ce que je crois*, he accepted without question. His early
teachers, content to allow their pupils' religious habits to remain
as conservative as possible, saw no need to stimulate critical
perception, and did their best to shield them from all possible
sources of harm: 'Nous étions élevés en vase clos. Le souci
dominait nos éducateurs de nous épargner tous les contacts; les
mauvais maîtres, les mauvais livres, les mauvaises compagnies
nous menaçaient de toutes parts.'[2]

This absorption in religion was matched in Mauriac's youth,
by an equally important desire to identify himself with nature
and with the make-believe worlds of literature. In *Bordeaux* he
describes his eagerness to lose himself in the throbbing natural
world of the *landes*: 'Assis sur un tronc de pin, au milieu d'une
lande, dans l'étourdissement du soleil et des cigales, ivre à la
lettre d'être seul, je ne pouvais pourtant pas supporter cette
confrontation avec moi-même à laquelle j'avais tant aspiré, et ne
me retrouvais que pour me perdre, pour me dissoudre dans la
vie universelle.'[3] Similarly one recalls the young narrator of

---

[1] *NMI*, p. 71.   [2] *BD*, O.C. t. xi. 441–2.   [3] Op. cit., O.C. t. iv. 162.

Préséances who 'isolé du monde, immobile comme un fakir, [devenait] le héros de mille drames'[1] or Gabriel Gradère who, miraculously freed for a moment of his many anxieties, becomes absorbed into the natural world around him.[2]

Retrospective criticism of these early years is relatively easy of course and Mauriac is somewhat unjust when, in 1960, he contends that during the years before he went to Paris he was 'un enfant spirituellement abandonné'.[3] He was only spiritually abandoned in the sense that the highly emotional religion which he had automatically and unquestioningly accepted was already beginning to crumble within him. The influence of Barrès, his own imitative 'culte du moi', and the First World War all combined to make his doubts and problems more acute. His *Journal d'un homme de trente ans* shows him gradually awakening to problems with a wider context of reference than the *Sillon*, yet even when war opens his eyes to the predicament of the human race as a whole his principal concern is still very much with his personal position and feelings. He prefers solitude: 'Etre oublié dans cette retraite' he writes from Malagar in 1918, 'N'être relié au monde que par des œuvres. Certitude d'atteindre les cœurs du fond de ma solitude. Dire au reste du monde: *Noli me tangere*.'[4] As they developed, Mauriac's real problems were of a much more private nature. A threat to the stability of his marriage[5] and bitter criticism of his work undermined his whole life. Talking of this crisis today and writing about it in *Ce que je crois* and *Nouveaux Mémoires intérieurs,* he gives the impression that he was for a while dangerously close to a complete nervous breakdown: 'Pendant deux ou trois ans, je fus comme fou [. . .] J'errais à travers Paris, comme un chien perdu, comme un chien sans collier'[6] and the adjustments which Mauriac found himself required to make form the material for *Souffrances et bonheur du chrétien.*

The first part of this work, *Souffrances du pécheur*, was undertaken, says Mauriac, 'sans plaisir, comme l'un de ces devoirs

---

[1] Op. cit., O.C. t. x. 350. [2] *AN*, p. 32. [3] *NB-N*, p. 338.
[4] Op. cit., O.C. t. iv. 251.
[5] See, for example, *NMI*, p. 273, and the reference in C. Jenkins, *Mauriac*, London and Edinburgh, 1965, p. 2 note. [6] *CQJC*, p. 162 and p. 163.

imposés par les éditeurs aux dociles écrivains'. But, he goes on, it suddenly became central and meaningful for him and 'tout un destin cristallisait'.[1] In this essay Mauriac shows himself to be tormented by the purist idea that love is only truly conceivable as a private relationship with God. On a number of occasions we find him maintaining that not only is it impossible for man to share both divine and mortal love, but that by nature he is inevitably inclined to the latter: 'Existe-t-il un seul homme au monde qui, livré à toutes les délices de la chair, demeure en union avec Dieu? ... il peut exister dans le même homme des alternances de vie sensuelle et de vie spirituelle, mais ces deux vies ne coexistent jamais.'[2] At this stage in Mauriac's thinking love is regarded as a spiritual matter only; it must be, as he says elsewhere, 'dégagé de toute sexualité'. Such a vigorously severe attitude to love is a far cry from Lacordaire's proclamation that all love is legitimate since it is embraced in the love of God, yet the inevitable fact that love between mortals does exist and leads in many cases to marriage does nothing to alleviate Mauriac's bitterness. He regards marriage simply as another expression of human weakness, and one moreover which tricks its participants; even the fusion of bodies in the sexual act is a deceit:

Dans ce bref intervalle de l'union charnelle, nous avons cru n'être qu'un, et de nouveau nous sommes deux: ce corps, cet autre corps; ce mur, cette poitrine fermée, monde clos de chair et de sang autour duquel nous tournons, satellite misérable.[3]

Mauriac also delights in quoting Pascal who notoriously condemned marriage as 'La plus basse des conditions du Christianisme, vile et préjudiciable selon Dieu.' By 1931, however, the bitterness is tempered; marriage is an institution of the flesh and must remain, but can do so only as a poor imitation of man's relationship with God: 'nous savons qu'il n'est qu'une caricature de l'union divine'.[4] It still offers only incomplete satisfaction to each of the partners and its spiritual emptiness is echoed by physical frustration. There is a strong inference that marriage is simply a human arrangement which has developed from man's inability

---

[1] *Préface*, O.C. t. vii. 225–6.   [2] *SBC*, O.C. t. vii. 239.
[3] Ibid., p. 231.   [4] *J*, II. 191.

to live alone. Quite clearly one solution to this dilemma lies in celibacy and in a life of whole-hearted devotion to the execution of God's will on earth. We find this exemplified by Pierre Gornac (*Destins*), Alain Forcas (*Ce qui était perdu* and *Les Anges noirs*), and Xavier Dartigelongue (*L'Agneau*) who, subject to normal human desires, passions and temptations, can only evaluate and overcome them in the light of their higher love. Together with Xavier, Pierre and Alain would only love Dominique 'plus que personne en ce monde'.[1]

Such a solution, however, is hardly practicable and another, based on compromise, more easily takes its place. In *Bonheur du chrétien* Mauriac cautiously allows marriage some values:

Dans l'amour humain, il existe comme des permissions de bonheur, des exemptions brèves; et chacun se rappelle quelques havres de calme joie, une journée, un rapide voyage, petite île où reprend souffle, un instant, l'amour exténué,—comme lorsque, à bout de force, les oiseaux de passage, en plein océan, s'abattent sur un navire.[2]

But such moments are rare. The love between mortals which is implicit in marriage must not be worshipped as an absolute value; Lacordaire's dictum still applies and Mauriac makes very few references to marriage in which there are no attendant reservations.[3]

Mauriac's resolution of this problem, albeit founded on a compromise, not only lessened his private anxieties but gave new direction to his imaginative writing, and the attempt to consider the workings of Grace in the Catholic novels of the 1930s is as much a result of his having achieved personal satisfaction as it is of the criticism levelled against him by those like Gide or Maritain, who either considered his work to have been productive of an adverse moral effect or accused him of betraying his faith. A natural corollary to this reflection of his own spiritual dilemma is the value which Mauriac places on confession, and on the need for the society which he depicts, and by implication for society as

[1] *A*, p. 145.   [2] Op. cit., O.C. t. vii. 260.
[3] The most notable example of course is *Le Mystère Frontenac*, though even in this novel the positive values of marriage are only inferred. As we shall see the life shared by Jean-Louis and Madeleine is much more typical of Mauriac's usual depiction.

a whole, to become aware of its failings by facing up to and analysing them. Only then will it be in a position where it is worthy of Salvation. It is here that we find the repeated image of true and false values, of real and assumed identity, and Mauriac in his novels never tires of showing how bourgeois society allows material values to usurp all too readily the place that rightfully belongs to spiritual ones, and that self-examination is markedly absent from this world. Mauriac's own desire for security as a boy could, of course, be regarded as being itself typical of this society, but even though the probings of his own conscience, particularly in matters of religious belief, enabled him to avoid much of the conservative complacency of his fellow *bordelais*, he has nevertheless always shared their basic mistrust of innovation and superficiality. Paris in particular is harshly treated, though his description of its 'pleasures' are more than pieces of satire of varying success and Mauriac hints at the real point of such sketches and observations in this remark from *Paroles catholiques*: 'le trait commun à tous les extrémismes philosophiques ou littéraires en faveur aujourd' hui, tels par exemple le surréalisme, c'est que ce sont des mystiques privées de Dieu et que ces mystiques sans Dieu sont à base de désespoir'.[1] One recalls too Fabien in *Le Mal* who contemplating the artistic world of Paris 'se demandait si leur art n'était pas la forme de leur désespoir'.[2] There is, however, perhaps no better example of those who indulge in such 'mystiques sans Dieu', those who substitute one type of worship for another, than Mauriac's brief description of the couples dancing in the night-club in *Le Désert de l'amour*:

Comme le jazz reprenait haleine, les hommes se détachèrent des femmes et ils battaient des mains, puis les tendaient vers les nègres, avec le geste des suppliants—comme si leur vie eût dépendu de ce vacarme; les noirs miséricordieux se déchaînèrent alors, et les éphémères, soulevés par le rythme, volèrent derechef, accolés.[3]

Such intoxicated behaviour described in language more usually associated with a religious context—'les tendaient vers les nègres, le geste des suppliants, miséricordieux'—is at the same time rendered contemptible, by the two words 'éphémères' and 'accolés'. There can be no doubt about Mauriac's intention; such shallow pleasures as these do exert the power of a primitive religion over society. Such failings, however, are not confined to the corrupt life of the city alone. As we shall see they are only one example of a general escapism, of the need society feels to set up and worship false idols in an attempt to hide its spiritual worthlessness not only from others but also from itself. It is all one massive cloak of 'mauvaise foi', and only occasionally does an individual appear to challenge this existence, riddled as it is with the rites and taboos of the family unit and its sacred property. Yet such efforts as these are in human terms doomed to failure; even Thérèse Desqueyroux finds that society is stronger than she is and that it eventually overcomes her. 'Ne penses-tu?' she asks Bernard, 'que la vie de notre espèce ressemble déjà terriblement à la mort?'[1] The only possible way out is in the direction of God; only then will she, or anyone else, discover 'la fin de la nuit'.

This draws Mauriac back towards the obsessive problem of how to convince his audience of the reality of God's love, of how to depict not examples of Grace having been effective but of Grace actually taking possession of an individual, such as Louis in *Le Nœud de vipères* or Gradère in *Les Anges noirs*, and leading him to the point of Salvation. The solution lies in the natural world which Mauriac knew around him as a boy and which is so vividly and sensually depicted in his poetry. The fusion of these two worlds—pagan and Christian—is not simply a romantic adornment, for gradually it is moulded to form the very substance of his achievement as a Catholic novelist:

Il fut un temps où je ne recevais d'elle [la nature] d'autre leçon que la passivité du fleuve, que l'abandon de l'arbre courbé, redressé, creusé dans l'épaisseur de ses feuilles, obéissant à tout souffle. Vais-je me troubler encore? Quelle est cette langueur? Mais non, je vois maintenant ce qu'alors mon œil intérieur se refusait à découvrir: des clochers jalonnent le fleuve invisible; la plaine n'est qu'un sillon immense où ce n'est pas le grain qui meurt, ni même le froment qui mûrit, mais où un Pain caché, enseveli, vivant, se multiplie. Il suffit qu'il soit là pour sanctifier cette Cybèle appesantie et déjà ivre avant toute vendange. Si

[1] *TD*, p. 80.

le vent courbe les branches, c'est devant les villages serrés autour d'un tabernacle. A vol d'oiseau l'hostie n'est guère plus eloignée de moi qu'elle ne serait dans une cathédrale. Cybèle est purifiée par Celui que je ne vois pas; elle se referme sur Lui; elle Le cache sous des pierres, dans des feuilles; elle le contient: l'ostensoir a des rayons de vignes et de forêts.[1]

The material was at hand from his earliest years, but the apprenticeship as a novelist was prolonged. Personal anxieties and problems caused him on more than one occasion to question his position as a novelist both in relation to his public and to the material of his books, and the debate traced in particular through *Le Roman*, *Dieu et Mammon*, and *Le Romancier et ses personnages* states his intentions against which his achievement must be measured.

During the twentieth century in France three outstanding Catholic writers and thinkers in particular have presented diverging theses on the subject of religious art. Léon Bloy in 1905 expressed the view that while a writer can be a Christian it is impossible to produce Christian art:

L'Art est un parasite aborigène de la peau du premier serpent. Il tient de cette extraction son immense orgueil et sa suggestive puissance. Il se suffit à lui-même comme un Dieu et les couronnes fleuronnées des princes, comparées à sa coiffure d'éclairs, ressemblent à des carcans. Il est aussi réfractaire à l'adoration qu'à l'obéissance et la volonté d'aucun homme ne l'incline vers aucun autel. Il peut consentir à faire l'aumône du superflu de son faste à des temples ou à des palais, quand il y trouve à peu près son compte, mais il ne faut pas lui demander un clin d'œil surérogatoire. . . .

Il peut se rencontrer d'exceptionnels infortunés qui soient, en même temps, des artistes et des chrétiens, mais il ne saurait y avoir un art chrétien.[2]

As far as the novel is concerned, Bloy bases his argument on the content, though it does not necessarily follow that the effect of a novel will be harmful simply because it does not treat wholesome

[1] *SBC*, O.C. t. vii. 266.
[2] Quoted by J. Maritain in *Art et Scolastique*, Paris, 1920, p. 221, note 142.

subjects. Indeed, Bloy's own work produced a considerable religious awakening among his readers in spite of its often turgid and sombre portrayal of life; 'il y en a qui demandent le baptême après m'avoir lu. Quelle sanction divine à mes violences.'[1] His violence and anger, he argues, are only 'l'effervescence de ma pitié'. An equally dogmatic convert to Catholicism, Paul Claudel, seems on the other hand to maintain that the content of a work must be closely allied to religious faith. On 20 January 1904 he wrote to Gabriel Frizeau: 'le dessein dans lequel sont écrits tous mes livres [. . .] est de le [Dieu] mieux connaître et de le mieux aimer et de le mieux faire connaître et aimer'.[2] Ten years later at the time of his rupture with Gide over Les Caves du Vatican he expressed the same idea. Moreover for Claudel literature exerts a strong persuasive force and whatever deals with unwholesome subjects must be harmful: 'Ne vous rendez-vous pas compte de l'effet que peuvent avoir vos livres sur de malheureux jeunes gens?[3] he asks Gide. And a few days later: 'La littérature fait parfois un peu de bien, mais elle peut faire surtout beaucoup de mal.'[4] One might, of course, question Claudel's integrity in all this and find substantial contradictory evidence in some of the ambiguous sexual-religious symbolism that is a standard feature of much of his own work. Sartre as well would argue against this view, claiming that Claudel was ignoring the reader's freedom, and that to have any significance at all, a novel must depend on the reader's reactions.

It is, however, one of the most respected and influential of French Catholic intellectuals, Jacques Maritain, who has suggested one solution, and at the same time has had most influence over the development of Mauriac as a Catholic writer. Maritain's cardinal rule is that the writer must never adopt a Christian pose, nor must he surrender his faith for the sake of his art:

Ne séparez pas votre art de votre foi. Mais laissez distinct ce qui est distinct. N'essayez pas de confondre de force ce que la vie unit si bien. Si vous faisiez de votre esthétique un article de foi, vous gâteriez votre

---

[1] Quoted by J. Maritain, in Quelques pages sur Léon Bloy, Paris, 1927, p. 17.
[2] Correspondance, 1857–1938, Paris, 1952, p. 32.
[3] Correspondance, 1899–1926, Paris, 1949, p. 217.
[4] Ibid., p. 221.

foi. Si vous faisiez de votre dévotion une règle d'opération artistique, ou si vous tourniez le souci d'édifier en un procédé de votre art, vous gâteriez votre art.'[1]

For Maritain art and religious faith must complement one another naturally; it is not what the artist depicts that is important but how he does so:

La question essentielle n'est pas de savoir si un romancier peut ou non peindre tel ou tel aspect du mal. La question essentielle est de savoir à *quelle hauteur* il se tient pour faire cette peinture, et si son art et son cœur sont assez purs, et assez forts, pour le faire sans connivence. Plus le roman descend dans la misère humaine, plus il exige d'un romancier des vertus surhumaines.[2]

While not as rigorous as Claudel in his interpretation of the view that the religious novelist has a certain responsibility towards his public, Maritain does think along the same lines. But it is his particular point about the author's involvement, about connivance, that affects Mauriac most considerably.

These views are only briefly sketched out, but do give some indication of the predominant attitudes adopted by leading French Catholic intellectuals. Mauriac's own theories of novel writing show that he was certainly aware of them but never wholly convinced. At no time, for example, does he share Claudel's view that the novelist is a member of a privileged sect whose function it is to interpret and convey the secrets of existence.[3] Certainly he hopes that the faith that is central to his own life will permeate his novels and become apparent to others, but achievement often belies intention. In spite of the fact that Mauriac has always maintained that his novels are firmly centred on his faith, his problem has continually been one of presentation. For the most part he would appear to agree with his fellow novelist Georges Bernanos who, in an interview with Frédéric Lefèvre, pointed out that religious faith was a highly personal matter and could not be translated into the cold reality of print: 'Le catholicisme n'est pas une règle seulement imposée du dehors: c'est la règle de la vie, c'est la vie même. [...] L'expérience vécue

---

[1] *Art et Scolastique*, p. 98.   [2] Ibid., p. 233, note 163.
[3] *Correspondance*, 1899–1926, p. 54.

de l'amour divin n'est pas du domaine du roman.'[1] In 1924 in *Sous le soleil de Satan* Bernanos, on his own admission, attempted to revitalize weakening Catholic faith. His powerful melodramatic depictions of evil and corruption are strongly reminiscent of Barbey d'Aurevilly and Bloy but so challenge the spiritual purity represented by the abbé Donissan that Bernanos was accused by some of Manichaeism. The problem of the novel about Grace still remained, yet when it did appear *La Joie* (with the exception of *Un Crime* written in strained circumstances to swell his income) was the least successful of his works albeit the most pure and the most mystical; *angoisse* once again, it seemed, had proved easier to write about than *joie*. But Bernanos moved on and in the *Journal d'un curé de campagne*, accepted by the majority of his critics as his greatest novel, he fuses Grace with human psychology so successfully that he appears on occasions to have found a solution.[2]

In 1924 Mauriac had already arrived at much the same conclusion as Bernanos. At the very end of *Le Mal* we read: 'Quel artiste oserait imaginer les cheminements et les ruses de la Grâce, protagoniste mystérieux? C'est notre servitude et notre misère de ne pouvoir peindre sans mensonge que les passions.' Unlike Bernanos, however, he could not rid himself of the obsession, and in spite of a number of lengthy discussions it was not until his final novels and in *L'Agneau* in particular that he attempted to alter his technique. By this time it proved to be too late.

Mauriac's objection to the description of himself as 'un romancier catholique' must be considered to be aimed at those preconceived notions about religious writers and their work, which present them as monuments of edification. As we have already noted, in recent years he has allowed that of all his novels only *Ce qui était perdu*, *Le Nœud de vipères*, and *Les Anges noirs* can be considered 'Catholic'.[3] Significantly of course these are all post-conversion novels, and while this crisis in Mauriac's life does mark a change in his writing, it is one of intention rather than technique

[1] *Le Crépuscule des vieux*, Paris, 1956, p. 68 and p. 82.

[2] See my article 'The Art of Georges Bernanos: the *comtesse* episode, in the *Journal d'un curé de campagne*', *French Review*, Vol. 45, No. 5, April 1969, pp. 673–82.

[3] O.C. t. iii. *Préface*, p. II.

or material. As Professor Stratford writing of the 1930 novels remarks: 'They did not vary greatly in theme or in tone from those that went before and, again, the unity of Mauriac's vision was the striking thing, not the development. His general subject was still the world, the flesh and the devil, and there were, as usual, more vipers than doves among his characters.'[1] Indeed it was the intention behind the novels which prompted so much criticism of Mauriac's work in the twenties, causing him considerable personal anxiety. As such it is an inseparable part of the debate crystallized in *Souffrances et bonheur du chrétien*, but *Le Roman, Dieu et Mammon*, and *Le Romancier et ses personnages* are worth our attention to see how in theory Mauriac attempted to work out this problem as a writer, and to what extent he was influenced both by current literary ideas and by criticism.

The general upheaval which took place in France after the First World War in literature and the arts is by now a well known and accepted fact. Of all names and works which stand out immediately as pointers, one of great, perhaps the greatest, significance is that of Freud. His *Introduction to Psychoanalysis* translated into French for the first time in 1922 excited a great deal of curiosity, but often only because it provided an apparently scientific justification for similar matter which had already found its way into literature. Proust in particular had pushed the novel away from the traditional, positivist writing of the nineteenth century, pursuing instead the irrational and intimate aspects of human nature. Russian authors also made their impact on the French literary scene, and greatly benefited from the type of stimulus given, for example, by Gide's series of lectures on Dostoievsky. These elements combined to create a literary climate which influenced the work of almost every ambitious young novelist trying to establish himself in the eyes of the critical world. One such writer who flashed briefly but brilliantly across the scene was Raymond Radiguet, and it is not surprising to find that Mauriac gives him a place beside the more illustrious if traditional company of Molière, Voltaire, Rousseau, Flaubert, and others in *Mes Grands Hommes*. In particular Mauriac admires the young novelist for having written in *Le Bal du Comte d'Orgel*, a

[1] Stratford, p. 166.

novel which, in Radiguet's own words, is based 'non aux événements extérieurs, mais à l'analyse de sentiments'. Such admiration, however, can be considered little more than fashionable; more relevant is Mauriac's friendship with Jacques Rivière, who was already a close friend of Gide, in contact with Claudel, tortured by problems of religious faith and at the very hub of the artistic and literary world. In a series of articles entitled *Le Roman d'aventure*[1] Rivière not only offers his own proposals for the form which he believes the novel should adopt but clearly looks forward to Mauriac's theories as they first appear in *Le Roman*.

Dismissing Romantic literature as 'une sorte de monstre dans l'histoire de la littérature'[2] productive of works which offer only 'la façade de l'œuvre de génie',[3] and Classical writing as so contrived and contained that nothing 'se réserve le droit de grandir encore',[4] Rivière goes on to discuss his conception of the new form for the novel. From *Le Roman d'aventure* two main points emerge. The first is the necessity for length and an abundance of detail if the novel is to succeed. So involved can it become in fact that 'On perd de vue sa direction, son fil; avec ses prolongements de toutes parts, elle ressemble à ces êtres marins qui avancent dans n'importe quel sens.'[5] No incidental material need be pruned away: 'rien ne lui est plus utile que l'inutile'.[6] The second point is that characters must enjoy complete autonomy, so much so in fact that both reader and author remain ignorant of the directions which the actions and emotions of the characters will take: 'celui qui l'a créé est là à côté de nous dans la même ignorance et dans la même attente que nous'.[7] Such improvements are to be in no way limited to novels dealing merely with material events; there is every opportunity for a psychological novel to follow exactly the same pattern. The reader (and author) should have no more indication or notion of the development of a character's mind than he does of events. He should be able to identify himself with the character, experiencing and discovering emotions and events only at the same time as he does. Predictably

---

[1] See the *Nouvelle Revue Française*, May, June, July 1939. These are reproduced as a single article in *Nouvelles Etudes*, Paris, 1947, pp. 235–83.
[2] Le roman d'aventure, *Nouvelles Etudes*, p. 251. [3] Ibid., p. 253.
[4] Ibid., p. 255. [5] Ibid., p. 268. [6] Ibid., p. 269. [7] Ibid., p. 271.

enough, Rivière finds that only Dostoievsky has achieved this, and consequently presents him as a kind of literary prototype. In all, the achievement of the *roman d'aventure* lies in its power to hold the reader in suspense, to involve him in the very uncertain nature of life itself:

Justement c'est l'abandon à l'inquiétude; en lisant un roman d'aventure, nous nous livrons sans réserve au mouvement du temps et de la vie, nous acceptons d'éprouver jusqu'au fond de nos moelles cette question obscure et infatigable qui pousse et travaille tous les êtres vivants, nous nous remettons, pieds et poings liés, à la misérable et merveilleuse anxiété de nous y sentir pour un instant complètement arrachés.[1]

Even if Rivière's theories did not directly influence the writing of people like Radiguet and Mauriac, his essay did at least formulate ideas that were current and fashionable at the time. His suggestions that the writer should expose the innermost workings of the mind found favour with Mauriac, even if he did not choose to extend this into a Catholic notion of confession, and towards the discovery of God's presence in every individual.

From the very beginning of his own discussion of the novel in *Le Roman* Mauriac, as we might expect, involves religion; literary creation is directly comparable to divine creation:

Le romancier est, de tous les hommes, celui qui ressemble le plus à Dieu; il est le singe de Dieu. Il crée des êtres vivants, il invente des destinées, les tisse d'événements et de catastrophes, les entrecroise, les conduit à leur terme. [. . .] la plupart des gens de lettres veuillent se persuader qu'ils ont reçu, en naissant, le don divin.[2]

The novelist has convinced himself that he occupies a position of omniscience and omnipotence; he has as much right to explore and expose the workings of his characters' minds as he has to create the situations in which they find themselves. At the same time, however, Mauriac argues that the novelist is obliged to explore new material for his work. Present society, he believes, lacks the type of internal conflict it once had to offer; it bends before events and moreover fails to provide the binding force once offered by religious faith. As Jacques Rivière wrote despairingly to Claudel as early as 1907: 'je vois que le christianisme

[1] Ibid., p. 278.   [2] Op. cit., O.C. t. viii. 263.

se meurt',[1] and Bernanos nearly twenty years later: '[...] la guerre nous a contraints à une révision complète des valeurs morales.'[2] One possibility Mauriac agrees could lie in the traditional device of having the novel mirror society. Indeed even such relatively minor novelists as Paul Morand or Drieu la Rochelle were to do this with some measure of success, but such efforts, Mauriac maintains, are ultimately fruitless. The novelist must realize that he is faced with a society that is 'terriblement appauvrie du côté de l'âme'[3] and must search in new directions:

[...] le romancier s'aventure, avec une audace croissante, sur des terres maudites où naguère encore nul n'aurait osé s'engager.'[4]

For some Freud had already pointed a way, though for others like Bernanos and Mauriac himself, Freud and psychoanalytical methods were only a poor substitute for what Maritain had already defined three years earlier in *Trois Réformateurs* as 'la science sacerdotale du Christ'. Yet in spite of what he may say the influence of this method—perhaps filtered from Rivière's writings —is clearly present in Mauriac's own theories and indeed in his novels.

Initially Mauriac has adopted a traditional position, taking for the bulk of his material provincial life as he knows it with all its peculiar characteristics and social requirements. He is, however, also aware of the severe limitations of this method, even though the depiction of provincial life in the manner of Balzac might remain for some critics the necessary criterion for success. For Mauriac success lies in innovation. Man should no longer be considered in terms of a social group; he is an individual to be studied in his own right:

il est certain qu'au delà de la vie sociale, de la vie familiale d'un homme, au delà des gestes que lui imposent son milieu, son métier, ses idées, ses croyances, existe une plus secrète vie: et c'est souvent au fond de cette boue cachée à tous les yeux que gît la clef qui nous le livre enfin tout entier.[5]

All social characteristics, all façades must be swept aside in an

---

[1] *Correspondance*, Paris, 1963, p. 31.   [2] *Le Crépuscule des vieux*, p. 11.
[3] R, O.C. t. viii. 267.   [4] Ibid., p. 269.   [5] Ibid., p. 273.

attempt to 'Mettre en lumière le plus individuel d'un cœur, le plus particulier, le plus distinct [. . .].[1] Unfortunately it has been characteristic of novelists since Balzac to provide their characters with a 'passion dominante' or, as Stendhal defined it, a 'passion maîtresse', and not until Dostoievsky was this fashion challenged. Echoing Rivière, Mauriac argues that the Russian depicts not types but 'des créatures de chair et de sang, chargées d'hérédités, de tares; sujets à des maladies; capables de presque tout en bien comme en mal et de qui on peut tout attendre, tout craindre, tout espérer'.[2] Dostoievsky's characters are men and women like ourselves whose actions frequently deny all logical explanation: 'des chaos vivants, des individus si contradictoires que nous ne savons que penser d'eux'.[3]

Already two years before in a *Préface* written for Bernard Barbey's novel *La Maladère*, Mauriac had made the same point:

Nous ne sommes plus de ceux qui sous couleur de débrouiller les motifs des actions des hommes, imposaient à leurs personnages cet enchaînement de raisons dont le mécanisme enchante le Français né logicien. Mais la logique de la vie se moque de cette fameuse logique, car elle est l'illogisme même : nous ne sommes plus des romanciers raisonneurs.[4]

Here as in *Le Roman* Mauriac claims that the novel has been governed by certain standard formulae, and, while the value of such writing is undeniable, the time has come for a change in both technique and direction. What is needed now is a movement towards 'l'illogisme, l'indétermination, la complexité des êtres vivants'.[5] At this point Mauriac reverts to the theme of the opening paragraphs of *Le Roman*—the comparison between the novelist and his characters with God and his creation—though he modifies his ideas in order to introduce the theological notion of free-will. The novelist must be allowed absolute freedom of choice in what he depicts, but he must also avoid any kind of preconceived plan. This would only result in predetermination, a kind of literary Jansenism. To illustrate his point Mauriac draws on his own experience, describing the free-will that his characters must enjoy for him to be satisfied with his work:

---

[1] Ibid., p. 274.   [2] Ibid., p. 275.   [3] Ibid., p. 275.
[4] Op. cit., Paris, 1926.   [5] R, O.C. t. viii. 276.

lorsque l'un de mes héros avance docilement dans la direction que je lui ai assignée, lorsqu'il accomplit toutes les étapes fixées par moi, et fait tous les gestes que j'attendais de lui, je m'inquiète; cette soumission à mes desseins prouve qu'il n'a pas de vie propre, qu'il n'est pas détaché de moi, qu'il demeure enfin une entité, une abstraction; je ne suis content de mon travail que lorsque ma créature me résiste, lorsqu'elle se cabre devant les actions que j'avais résolu de lui faire commettre [...] Je ne suis jamais tant rassuré sur la valeur de mon ouvrage que lorsque mon héros m'oblige à changer la direction de mon livre, me pousse, m'entraîne vers des horizons que d'abord je n'avais pas entrevus.[1]

In spite of the theological analogy, when it is defined in these terms, Mauriac's position is really no more than the fashionable one so adequately summarized by Jacques Rivière; when he moves on to consider what he refers to as 'le côté moral du problème', however, his concern for religion becomes increasingly noticeable and alters his perspective. Moreover the tone of the work changes from a straightforward critical essay to a piece of self-justification.

Once more Mauriac finds himself in agreement with Bernanos when he argues that in limiting himself solely to a depiction of his characters' sensuality a novelist can offer an incomplete picture only. This is where Proust has failed. His exploration of the unconscious, the 'terres inconnues' of human nature is to be admired, but unlike Dostoievsky he has failed to lead his characters to redemption. They express no 'goût de la pureté et de la perfection, la faim et la soif de la justice' which, according to Mauriac, form an essential part of the 'patrimoine humain',[2] and which it is the novelist's duty to depict. In displaying such concern for the content and the effect of novel writing Mauriac is here indirectly participating in the dispute which had already separated Claudel and Gide. Accused of betraying his faith in his novels, of showing too strong a preference for the murkier side of human nature, Mauriac reacts with some violence. For him every analysis of human nature and passions must lead to the discovery of God. This, for Mauriac, is an article of faith: the yearning for purity and perfection, which he contends is an

[1] Ibid., pp. 278–9.   [2] Ibid., p. 280.

essential part of human nature, witnesses, for him, the presence of God's Grace.

Without drawing our attention too overtly to the fact that Dostoievsky is also a 'Catholic novelist' Mauriac, by using the Russian author and his work as a model, moves into a position of defence and justification of his own work. To ignore the less pleasant aspects of human nature completely is certainly no guarantee that their influence will be removed. On the other hand the Catholic novel is not a handbook of virtue, 'celui qui ne nous entretient que de bons sentiments',[1] an edifying work which 'nous laisse l'impression d'une chose arrangée, montée de toutes pièces'.[2] Maritain's solution, for the novelist to depict whatever he wishes 'sans connivance' is referred to early in Le Roman, but it is rejected as unnecessary. For Mauriac all exploration of human nature is justified since ultimately it leads to 'le Royaume de Dieu qui soit au-dedans de nous'.[3] Unfortunately, if inevitably, however, Mauriac, like Bernanos, presents his case from the novelist's viewpoint, one which is not necessarily shared by his critical audience. Preconceived notions of what should constitute a Catholic novel are difficult to remove, and both writers were obliged to suffer a good deal of hostile criticism.

Mauriac's next work which contributes in any detail to this problem is Dieu et Mammon, written in the following year. Most directly this essay is an answer to an open letter from Gide which appeared in the Nouvelle Revue Française in 1928 and in which Mauriac is accused of allowing in his work 'ce compromis rassurant qui permette d'aimer Dieu sans perdre de vue Mammon'.[4] In the Préface to a recent reissue of Dieu et Mammon Mauriac claims that it contains some of the most significant pages he has ever written, and certainly if the impassioned tone of much of what he says could be taken as evidence there is little reason to doubt him. Written in 1929 Dieu et Mammon forms an essential part of the spiritual debate which Mauriac largely made public in Souffrances et bonheur du chrétien, but as a commentary on his development as a novelist it marks an intermediary stage only. Mauriac admits the validity of Gide's criticism, and attempts to

---

[1] Le Crépuscule des vieux, p. 83.   [2] R, O.C. t. viii. 282.
[3] Ibid., p. 283.   [4] Op. cit., p. 331.

justify himself on two fronts—the first his Catholic upbringing which, as we have seen, conditioned his attitude to religious matters at an early age, and the second his vocation as a writer. Literature in a sense was therapeutic.

The dilemma of the novelist expressed in *Dieu et Mammon* echoes *Le Roman*: edification and moralizing must be avoided at all costs and give way to the 'connaissance de l'homme'. 'Au vrai, les écrivains qui truquent le réel pour édifier le lecteur et qui peignent des êtres sans aucune vérité pour être sûrs de n'être pas immoraux, n'atteignent que rarement leur but.'[1] Much, he maintains, depends on the reader's reaction and as evidence cites once again his own Christian attitude to Proust. He also re-examines and rejects Maritain's arguments about connivance: it is impossible not to connive at a character's actions since successful character portrayal in a novel depends above all on an intimate fusion of creator (novelist) and created. The novelist, Catholic or otherwise, is trapped by his profession:

L'ambition du romancier moderne est en effet d'appréhender l'homme tout entier avec ses contradictions et avec ses remous. Il n'existe pas dans la réalité de belles âmes à l'état pur: on ne les retrouve que dans les romans, je veux dire: dans les mauvais romans.[2]

One inevitable response to this is obviously to write about saints. Again Mauriac forestalls his critic, but in so doing serves only ironically to emphasize the problem that haunts him throughout the twenties—the impossibility of introducing Grace into the novel:

Chaque fois que l'un de nous a voulu réinventer, dans une fiction romanesque, les cheminements de la Grâce, ses luttes, sa victoire, nous avons toujours eu l'impression de l'arbitraire et du truquage. Rien de moins saisissable que le doigt de Dieu dans le cours d'une destinée. Non qu'il soit invisible, mais ce sont des touches si délicates qu'elles disparaissent dès que nous les voulons fixer. Non, Dieu est inimitable, il échappe à la prise du romancier. [...] L'échec de la plupart des romanciers qui ont voulu donner la vie à des saints, vient peut-être de ce qu'ils se sont exténués à peindre des êtres sublimes, angéliques, inhumains, alors que leur chance unique aurait été de s'attacher à

[1] *DM*, O.C. t. vii. 310.   [2] Ibid., p. 315.

mettre en lumière ce que la sainteté laisse subsister de misérablement humain dans une créature humaine et qui est le domaine propre du romancier.[1]

Three years later when he welcomed René Bazin to the Académie Française, Mauriac repeated the same ideas and the very same words, but already in *Dieu et Mammon*, he was moving towards the clearer expression of his situation discussed in *Le Romancier et ses personnages* in 1933. By justifying his own faith in the early part of *Dieu et Mammon*, Mauriac has moved to a point where he views all in a Christian perspective; he makes no allowance for the non-Catholic writer. If not openly discussed, Grace will be implied even by its absence:

Ainsi l'un et l'autre race d'esprits, selon des modes différents, se soumet ou résiste à la Grâce.[2]

Dieu et Mammon with its tone of justification and even, at times, of self-defence is not Mauriac's final word on the problem however. Indeed the exclusion of this essay from Volume VIII of his complete works—which according to Mauriac throws most light on his development as a novelist—suggests that it relates more directly to his spiritual development than to his career as a man of letters, even though the two were so closely linked. *Le Romancier et ses personnages*, published in 1933, opens with a passage of blunt self-castigation, considerably modifies the claims made five years previously in *Le Roman*, and, while retaining the central notion of a Christian attitude to imaginative writing, taken as a whole is much more pessimistic in outlook.

From the very beginning Mauriac rejects the analogy of literary creation with a divine *creatio ex nihilo*: 'Les personnages qu'ils [les romanciers] inventent ne sont nullement créés, si la création consiste à faire quelque chose de rien.'[3] Any creation of character in imaginative writing, any attempt at reproducing reality is in fact only a manipulation of what the novelist sees and knows within a certain perspective. It is inevitable, moreover, that the novelist will know how his characters develop: 'je n'ignore rien de ce qu'ils sentent, de ce qu'ils entendent à telle heure du jour et de la nuit, lorsqu'il sortent du vestibule et s'avancent sur le perron'.[1] The novelist may chose to exaggerate or falsify a given situation or characteristic and here, ironically enough, Mauriac echoes Gide, who claimed to explore facets of his own nature in the extreme actions and passions of his imagined characters, and contradicts the ideas he had so enthusiastically championed in *Le Roman* where he rejected the claims of certain modern novelists to portray man in all his individual complexity. Even Dostoievsky has failed: 'L'individu, tel que l'étudie le romancier, est une fiction. C'est pour sa commodité, et parce que c'est plus facile, qu'il peint des êtres détachés de tous les autres, comme le biologiste transporte une grenouille dans son laboratoire.'[2] Instead 'il ne sait qu'isoler de ce fourmillement et que fixer sous sa lentille une passion, une vertu, un vice qu'il amplifie démesurément.[3] [...] En un mot, dans l'individu, le romancier isole et immobilise une passion, et dans le groupe il isole et immobilise un individu. Et, ce faisant, on peut dire que ce peintre de la vie exprime le contraire de ce qu'est la vie: l'art du romancier est une faillite.'[4]

These final words, far removed from the buoyant enthusiasm of *Le Roman* can only be seen as the inevitable outcome of Mauriac's predicament. He has now reached a position where he is obliged to justify himself and his writing, and in doing so can only reiterate his claims of *Dieu et Mammon*. Since the novel is not an authentic reproduction but a transposition of reality the novelist can only hope to 'atteindre le vrai que par réfraction'.[5] The direct use of a character as a *porte-parole* can only lead to artificiality. Instead the novelist's own convictions must permeate the work as a whole in such a way that while they do not obtrude they are never obscured. The novelist, and above all the Catholic novelist, must centre his 'multiples contradictions autour d'un roc immuable; il faut que les puissances opposées de son être

[1] Ibid., p. 290.   [2] Ibid., p. 295.   [3] Ibid., p. 295.
[4] Ibid., p. 296.
[5] Ibid., p. 307. Cf, 'Les vivants ne ressemblent jamais à nos personnages inventés [...] il n'existe aucun roman qui participe à l'indétermination de la vie véritable.' *GAL*, Postface, p. 173 and p. 175.

cristallisent autour de Celui qui ne change pas. Divisé contre lui-même, et par là condamné à périr, le romancier ne se sauve que dans l'Unité, il ne se retrouve que quand il retrouve Dieu.'[1] For Mauriac the debate is closed, but the very method of his presentation leaves us with the central problem still unsolved. Throughout his discussion of Catholicism and literature Mauriac has elaborated two important considerations: on the one hand the need to consider the possible moral effect of a work, and on the other the technical problem of how to incorporate a personal conviction in a novel while at the same time avoiding any charge of didacticism. A further element which serves to confuse the issue is Mauriac's personal involvement; at no stage is he able to stand aside in order to consider Catholic literature objectively, and, since in the last resort all critical evaluations and opinions must be personal, his conclusions are legitimately questionable. Thus one might say that for them to be valid Mauriac's observations on Proust's work require a high degree of sympathy for Mauriac's general position. Here we come face to face with the crux of the whole issue. Mauriac may not be successful in convincing his readers of the need for them to share the Catholic faith, but by his own definition he is obliged to attempt to include his personal beliefs in his writing in such a way that they do not obtrude and hence become unacceptable. The inclusion of any such explanation or message as that contained in the letters with which Le Nœud de vipères closes or more noticeably the attempt to allegorize Christ's role in L'Agneau is the unsuccessful method of a writer who is preaching. His claim at the end of Le Romancier et ses personnages that his faith has always infused his work, that it is the 'roc immuable' around which his novels are written only begs the question. It is not enough that he should defend himself against the accusation of betraying his faith, for he has also to overcome the problem of depicting grace in such a way that even if it is rejected by some readers as an article of faith, at least it can be allowed as a necessary and unobjectionable feature of his writing. Mauriac's eternal problem has been to justify a statement made as early as 1924: 'Une certaine littérature d'édification falsifie la vie. La transcendence du christianisme

[1] Ibid., p. 308.

éclate dans sa conformité avec le réel: ne truquez donc pas le réel.' Catholic literature should be 'à la fois véridique et chaste'.[1] Unfortunately, as Mauriac found, this was all too frequently unrealizable.

[1] VMP, O.C. t. iv. 393.

2

THE FIRST STEPS

WITHOUT any points of direct comparison the problem of determining the influences, literary or otherwise, which have helped shape an author's work is of necessity a difficult one. Critical reaction to Mauriac's novels over the years has produced a substantial list of writers and thinkers to whom in theory he owes some debt—Pascal, Racine, Balzac, Maurice de Guérin, Barrès, Jammes, and Dostoievsky—and as we have seen in *Le Roman* and *Le Romancier et ses personnages*, and indeed as Mauriac has conveniently admitted elsewhere, such a list is not without its significance. At the same time, however, Mauriac is also recorded as having said that he has never been influenced by Proust. Unfortunately the inevitable outcome of any discussion of this nature would be that insoluble question of direct or indirect, conscious or unconscious influences, particularly acute in the case of a writer like Mauriac who was saturated with literature from an early age. Moreover the sheltered nature of his early years provided him with few external events on which he could draw instead for the substance of his work, a position that was of course to continue; as Michael Moloney has remarked, Mauriac is one of those writers who 'begin with themselves rather than the world outside'.[1] But Mauriac's private world has always been more than adequate, and while a detailed tracing of certain influences observable in his early stylistic techniques would provide a testing exercise, more important for the development of his later writing is the emergence of standard themes and personal convictions from the heavy layer of autobiographical material which dominates these formative years.

Of the early novels the very first, *L'Enfant chargé de chaînes* is in many ways the most interesting since it largely avoids the introverted atmosphere of the family which dominates so much

[1] M. Moloney, *François Mauriac, a critical study*, Denver, 1958, p. 160.

of Mauriac's subsequent imaginative writing, and deals instead with his brief relationship with Marc Sangnier's Social Catholic movement, the *Sillon*. Written between 1909 and 1912 and published in the following year *L'Enfant chargé de chaînes* has either been undeservedly ignored or dismissed by the majority of Mauriac's critics, as an unsuccessful first attempt. Jean-Paul Johanet, the novel's young hero, goes to Paris, as did Mauriac himself, to pursue studies in which he is only half-heartedly interested. He is melancholy, introspective and, like most of Mauriac's young protagonists, suffers from a surfeit of literature, in which he seeks an echo of his own emotions. Jean-Paul's melancholy and moments of romantic nostalgia, and his search for love both divine and human, colour the book so deeply that little or nothing of the vigour and penetration of later novels in the style of *Génitrix* or *Thérèse Desqueyroux* can be seen. Indeed, writing about *L'Enfant chargé de chaînes* in 1952, Mauriac himself admitted that 'ni mon style, ni mon atmosphère ne sont encore découverts',[1] and that even though largely autobiographical, his portrait of Jean-Paul was not a success.

The first few pages of the novel serve to introduce those characters who are to act as 'guides' for Jean-Paul during this formative period of his life—Marthe Balzon his cousin whose love for him is at first unreturned, Louis Fauveau, a sensual 'petit être nul', and Vincent Hiéron who is to introduce Jean-Paul to the movement *Amour et foi*. This introduction is followed by Jean-Paul's progress through the 'enterprise de démocratie chrétienne' by which he is gradually sickened. His failure to mould his own nature to accept the movement's values and ideals leads him to indulge at first in a life of debauchery with Fauveau and his friends, but finally to find comfort and relief in love for his cousin whom we can believe he will eventually marry.[2] Structurally, the book is easily divided—an introduction

[1] O.C. t. x. *Préface*, p. II.
[2] This reference may well have its connections with Mauriac's own intentions. In June 1913 he married Mlle Jeanne Lafont whom he had met the previous year. It was also in 1912 that Francis Jammes wrote to Mauriac about *ECC* in the following terms: 'La fin marque chez toi une telle compréhension de vie chrétienne que je te voudrais voir marié assez vite avec une jeune fille du genre de celle que tu dépeins' (20 July 1912), Choix de lettres de Francis Jammes à François Mauriac,

followed by two parts, the first of which deals with *Amour et foi*, the second with Jean-Paul's process of escape from the metaphorical chains of sadness and despair.

Although it is probably no more than a coincidence that Marc Sangnier in *Le Sillon, esprit et méthodes* speaks of the need to foster in oneself 'de la foi et de l'amour',[1] the comparison which can be made between *Amour et foi* and Sangnier's movement is not based entirely on vague Christian democratic ideals. There are in addition several points of material similarity.[2] Like the *Sillon*, the movement to which Jean-Paul is introduced centres its main activities on Paris, but attempts at the same time to spread 'la cause' through the provinces. Thus it is that Jean-Paul attends congress at Bordeaux, not only Mauriac's home town, but one of the main towns where Sangnier's movement was early established. The ambiguous letter received from Monseigneur Bonaud, containing '... des louanges mesurées, des réticences, des menaces déguisées sous une bénédiction',[3] recalls those received by Sangnier from Pius X: 'Restez fidèles à votre bannière et la promesse de l'Evangile s'accomplira en vous et vous regnerez...'[4] and 'Tout en nous réjouissant donc de votre force, Nous vous exhortons, dans vos œuvres et dans vos luttes, à placer votre confiance non pas en vos propres efforts, mais en la toute-puissance de Dieu.'[5] Here beneath apparent approval and

---

La Table Ronde, February 1956, p. 97. There is, however, no firm proof of this. Mauriac also writes in *NMI* (p. 237) of 'une mésaventure sentimentale' which occurred in 1911 and which is possibly reflected in Yves Frontenac's emotional problems in *MF*.

[1] Op. cit., p. 88.

[2] Further information concerning Social Catholicism and in particular *Le Sillon* is to be found in J. Caron, *Le Sillon et la Démocratie Chrétienne 1894–1910*, Paris, 1967; H. Rollet, *L'Action sociale des catholiques en France (1871–1914)*. Paris, 1958; J. de Fabrègues, *Le Sillon de Marc Sangnier*, Paris, 1964; J. E. Flower, 'Forerunners of the worker-priests', *Journal of Contemporary History*, Vol. 2, No. iv. Winter, 1967, pp. 183–99. Works written by people actively engaged in Social Catholicism at the time of the *Sillon* tend to be heavily prejudiced one way or the other. For example, E. Barbier, *Les Erreurs du Sillon*, Paris, 1906, writes against Sangnier; L. Cousin, *Vie et doctrine du Sillon*, Paris, 1906 and G. Hoog, *Histoire du Catholicisme Social en France*, 1871–1931, Paris, 1946, write in favour.

[3] *ECC*, O.C. t. x. 23.

[4] Quoted in *Le Sillon, esprit et méthodes*, Paris, 1905, pp. 70, 71 note 1.

[5] Quoted ibid., pp. 186–7.

encouragement lay the warning that Pius had clear ideas on the direction Sangnier's movement should adopt, if it were to retain his favour. And later on its condemnation this similarity with the *Sillon* is also to be found in the refusal of permission for priests and seminarists to attend the movement's meetings and to read its newspaper. It appears too in smaller details—the movement's violent red posters, the establishment of the 'cercles d'études' as centres of teaching and the portrait of 'Léon XIII bénissant'.

More important, however, is the indication of the development which *Amour et foi* has undergone. One of the principal reasons for the condemnation of the *Sillon* was the shift of emphasis from religious to predominantly political and social considerations. A similar trend seems to have occurred in *Amour et foi* and Vincent speaks with longing for the past and for freedom from the political squabbles and considerations that are now their concern:

C'était si beau autrefois, quand le monde nous ignorait, cette vie d'enthousiasme et de ferveur. On allait, tu te souviens, dans les banlieues.... On entrait dans les marchands de vin. Il y avait une conférence dans l'arrière-boutique. Tu parlais; on t'interrompait d'abord avec des farces ignobles, de gros rires. Peu à peu ces pauvres âmes s'éveillaient; une gravité inconnue apparaissait au fond des regards et tu pouvais alors parler du Christ.[1]

And a little later he remarks: 'Tout est changé, Jérôme; nous sommes une puissance, nous avons des journaux au service d'un programme politique.'[2]

In spite of this change in outlook, there remains throughout the movement an ardent desire to serve a never very well defined cause. This desire is injected into the lesser members of *Amour et foi* by the leader, Jérôme Servet, regarded by each of his disciples as a father and in some cases, judging from the dedications on the photographs in his room, as a representative of God himself.[3] Perhaps it is part of Mauriac's intention to demonstrate one of the basic weaknesses of *Amour et foi* when he shows that the relationship that Jérôme has with his followers is hierarchical in

[1] *ECC*, O.C. t. x. 23.   [2] Ibid., p. 24.
[3] Ibid., p. 51. See also G. Hoog, op. cit., p. 134.

nature. In spite of Sangnier's particular interpretation of the Hierarchy which, he maintained, allowed it to be integrated into a republican democracy, there is no evidence that he was very successful in its application. On the contrary he seems to have been convinced of the need for personal leadership and the success of the *Sillon* seems to have depended very much on this. This is also the case in *Amour et foi*. When Jérôme Servet first appears he is 'le maître' or 'le maître impérieux' and the imperious, paternal attitude he often adopts when he addresses his followers in turn produces a form of servility in them. Vincent, for example, 'stupéfait de son audace' when he suggests that *Amour et foi* is no longer the religious movement it had once been, is anxious to ingratiate himself again as quickly as possible with his leader,[1] while Marteau, another adoring follower, gazes at Jérôme with 'des yeux mouillés de bon chien'.[2] Ironically, once out of their leader's presence, Vincent and the new recruit Jean-Paul adopt the same patronizing tone and demand similar adoration from their own inferiors.[3]

The attraction *Amour et foi* has for Jean-Paul rests on two facts. The first of these is that the opportunity to meet a former school friend with whom he had much in common promises a relief from his normal desultory existence in Paris. Vincent, he believes, will introduce him to a new and rewarding way of life in which his personal sufferings and melancholy will be forgotten in his concern for matters of greater significance: 'Il se forge un idéal de vie grave et sérieuse, une vie toute pleine de religion et d'inquiétudes d'ordre social.'[4] The second and more important reason for the movement's attraction is that he is now afforded an opportunity to display both his superior bourgeois culture and education, and to exhibit his powers of charm and rhetoric. In other words Jean-Paul finds in *Amour et foi* not, as he at first believed, an opportunity for self-effacement and personal sacrifice for the benefit of others, but food for his own egoism. Marthe, thinking that she is making a wry comment about her relationship with Jean-Paul, ironically sums up his whole

[1] *ECC*, O.C. t. x. 24.   [2] Ibid., p. 30.
[3] See, for example, ibid., p. 22 and p. 44.
[4] Ibid., p. 28.

attitude: 'Oh! l'amour et toi ... —et elle eut un pauvre sourire.'[1]

However, in spite of his apparent acceptance of *Amour et foi*, even if it is for his own comfort, it is evident throughout *L'Enfant chargé de chaînes* that Jean-Paul is not at ease. We are constantly aware that his participation in the movement is a conscious effort. When he swears eternal friendship with the carpenter's boy Georges Élie, for example, he does so 'conscient de son mensonge'. He forces himself to ignore the self-evident truth that without an iron will the complete incompatibility of their characters and background makes a mockery of the whole affair. For the moment he finds glory in his surrender and in his strength of will to remain true to his 'vocation d'apôtre'.

It is Mauriac himself in one of his interventions later to become so plentiful and characteristic in his work who, at the end of Chapter VII, not only indicates his attitude to the character he has created but demonstrates the impossibility of the young man's situation once and for all:

Ainsi, docilement, le jeune homme baisse la tête pour recevoir le joug. Mais l'idéal vers quoi il marche lui demeure inconnu: il va en quelque sorte à reculons, les yeux levés sur les vieux dégoûts, sur les écœurements quotidiens. Il court à ce qui est peut-être la vérité, non parce que c'est la vérité mais pour se libérer des mornes tristesses qui le tuent. . . .[2]

The assumption of this persona, which he feels is necessary to enable him to blot out the 'mornes tristesses' of his life, is something which he can only temporarily achieve. Jean-Paul is ill at ease in this atmosphere of Social Catholicism and it is not surprising that he eventually becomes so sickened by *Amour et foi* that he takes no pains to conceal his scorn, either for his fellow workers or for the gullibility of those like Georges Élie, whose very attitude encourages the group's complacency: '[...] le soir après s'être exaspéré dans un cercle d'études, que de fois il s'était refugié dans sa chambre, ayant en lui le désir violent de se désencanailler.'[3] In addition the account we are given of a lecture delivered by Jean-Paul not only suggests how incompletely (and uncomprehendingly) the members of *Amour et foi* treated social

[1] Ibid., p. 32.   [2] Ibid., p. 30.   [3] Ibid., p. 38.

problems, but implies that Jean-Paul is not alone in his use of the trite stereotyped phrases:

'De même que le servage succéda à l'esclavage, pour être lui-même remplacé par le salariat moderne ... de même, camarades, nous devons croire que le patronat n'est pas éternel ...'

Jean-Paul dévide, sans presque y songer, le rouleau des vieilles formules démocratiques. Ses regards errent distraitement sur cet auditoire qui s'ennuie.[1]

Such criticism of both party and members is also discernible in the style of the novel. Certainly there is much that is not typical of the later Mauriac. In particular the conversations are often stilted and clumsy—those for example between Vincent Hiéron and Jérôme or Jean-Paul and Lulu.[2] We also find a considerable element of melodrama and sentimentality, especially in the effect Jérôme has over his disciples, and tearful reminiscences are common. Each of these aspects of the style in *L'Enfant chargé de chaînes* might well be attributed to inexperience, and yet one wonders if Mauriac is not attempting, in the second of these features at least, to parody Sangnier's own style as it appears for example in *Le Sillon, esprit et méthodes*. Here Sangnier's own emotional effusiveness is conveyed by frequently long and involved sentences which in fact have only an obvious point to make:

Sans doute, jamais celle-ci [l'œuvre du *Sillon*] n'a semblé plus nécessaire, jamais les prévisions humaines n'ont paru lui promettre de plus prochaines victoires: L'impuissance des vieux milieux reactionnaires, l'inutilité, chaque jour plus apparente, des coalitions pour l'œuvre de conquête, l'incapacité des socialistes au pouvoir à rester conséquents avec eux-mêmes et à ne pas trahir leurs déclarations anciennes, les équivoques où se traîne un gouvernement sectaire qui vit d'expédients et ne trouve que la haine anticléricale pour cimenter sa branlante majorité, les scandales et les dégoûts amoncelés partout, paraissent ouvrir un champ inespéré à l'ardeur vaillante d'une génération neuve qui brûle d'oublier toutes ces faiblesses et ces hontes pour écrire, à son tour, un peu d'histoire sur les pages de ce livre que les siècles tiennent toujours ouvert.[3]

[1] Ibid., pp. 36–7.
[2] See, for example, ibid., pp. 22–4, and pp. 69–71.
[3] Op. cit., pp. 88–90.

D1

This suggestion of parody is indeed given more weight when we examine Mauriac's descriptions of Jérôme. When he first appears he is presented as a man in whom physical vulgarity and spiritual purity are mingled, though it is implied that the latter is observable only to those who believe in Servet as a religious leader:

Il était seul, debout, le front collé contre la vitre, les poings enfoncés dans les poches d'un veston déformé et taché. Ceux qui l'aimaient ne voyaient pas sa cravate mal nouée, ses cheveux en désordre, cette bouche commune dans la face lourde, le cou énorme, les joues flasques et toujours mal rasées; ils ne voyaient que ses yeux admirables, un regard perdu, un regard qui atteignait les âmes et de belles mains longues et fines qui, dans un geste habituel, allaient sans cesse vers les mains de l'homme à conquérir, et, crispées, les retenaient d'une étreinte impérieuse . . . [1]

If we are to judge from photographs and descriptions of Sangnier elsewhere Mauriac appears to exaggerate, yet such a portrait, if it were isolated within the novel, might well reflect how Mauriac did actually see Sangnier. But there is as well the scene in which Mauriac evokes Jérôme's triumphant return from a pilgrimage at Lourdes where it becomes clear that Mauriac has other intentions:

Les camarades entouraient le lit de Jérôme qui devait regagner Paris dans la journée. Traversant Bordeaux après un long pèlerinage à Lourdes, il avait fait la veille une conférence publique. Vincent Hiéron, à genoux sur le tapis, ramassait pieusement le linge du grand homme, les flanelles humides encore d'une généreuse sueur; le maître lui avait enseigné que la plus humble besogne est magnifique, si on l'accomplit pour *la cause*. . . . [2]

The allusion to Christ is too obvious to be mistaken, though to ensure that it is not missed Mauriac unfortunately draws attention

---

[1] *ECC*, O.C. t. x. 22. A. Dansette (*Histoire religieuse de la France contemporaine*, Paris, 1951, p. 413 and p. 414) quotes Mauriac's description of Sangnier but suggests that it lacks an essential feature—the power Sangnier possessed to be loved by others. Amongst others Gillet, Rollet and Barbier all support Dansette. In view of the tribute which Mauriac pays to Sangnier in *NB-N*, pp. 336–8, however, it appears that he was fully aware of this gift. It would not help his case in *ECC* to show that he was ready to succumb to it. His aim here was to make Servet (Sangnier) appear slightly repulsive.

[2] Ibid., p. 50.

to it a few lines later. Nevertheless the juxtaposition of such pious language and 'les flanelles humides encore d'une généreuse sueur' reduces the tone of the passage to such an extent that even if blasphemy is avoided, caricature is not.

On various occasions Mauriac has remarked that he was known during this period of his life as a young man with a taste for satire, and in 1921 there appeared *Préséances*, his acrid satire of Bordeaux society. In *L'Enfant chargé des chaînes* it is not only Servet or by implication Sangnier who is caricatured and criticized; the target is much wider. Caricature could partly account for the sentimental effusiveness of the lesser members of *Amour et foi*. It also implies that Jean-Paul was for a time typical of the majority of Servet's followers, and that he was not alone in the reiteration of the 'vieilles formules démocratiques'. The whole programme of *Amour et foi* was no more successful for Jean-Paul than that of the *Sillon* for Mauriac, but the faults lay not so much with the party as with the individual concerned. Mauriac, though caricaturing much of what the *Sillon* stood for, offers no constructive suggestions for its repair, and that he should have reacted in this manner can be attributed in particular to the influence which a reading of Barrès had upon him and not a deep rooted conviction.[1]

From Mauriac's frequent reference to Barrès it is clear that it was the Academician's early work that influenced him most. In *La Recontre avec Barrès* he wrote:

Le vrai Barrès tenait tout entier à mes yeux dans les trois livres du *Culte du Moi*, dans deux romans: *L'Ennemi des Lois* et *Les Déracinés* et dans quelques pages d'*Amori et Dolori Sacrum* et de *Du Sang* (en particulier la nouvelle: *Un Amateur d'Ames*). A presque tout ce qu'il publia ensuite, et même à un grand livre comme *La Colline inspirée*, je ne me suis prêté que par devoir, et par gratitude.[2]

But however high his admiration for Barrès was by the time he left Bordeaux for Paris, it could not have received a greater stimulus than when, in 1910, Barrès took it upon himself to praise

---

[1] Mauriac has of course in later years given considerable support to much of what the *Sillon* stood for. See, for example, *PA*, pp. 27–8; *Le Figaro*, 5 June 1950, p. i; J, V. 52; *MP*, *Préface*, pp. 10–14.

[2] Op. cit., O.C. t. iv. 182.

Mauriac's first collection of poems, *Les Mains jointes*, in an article published by *L'Echo de Paris*. A brief extract from Mauriac's private diary given in *La Rencontre avec Barrès* indicates the extent to which he had imbibed Barrès' influence:

Ne vois chez les camarades des Chartes qui s'appliquent mieux que toi à leur tâche parce qu'il leur est plus facile de se borner, ne vois que des utilités professionnelles.

N'attache non plus d'importance aux spécialistes à qui tu t'es apparemment soumis. Ta fortune te permettra toujours de te délivrer d'eux lorsque leur joug deviendra plus lourd et plus injurieuse leur attitude ... Au retour de ce dîner où des jeunes gens prétentieux et bruyants t'énervèrent, pourquoi es-tu inquiet de l'effet que tu leur produisais? Jamais plus tu ne les reverras, ces inconnus au large rire blessant. Jamais plus tu ne renverseras un bibelot devant eux. ... Vis au sommet d'une tour d'indifférence. Qu'elle domine la plaine immense où campent les barbares. Dans cette tranquille nuit où siffle un peu ta lampe où l'indigeste dîner te trouble encore, prends conscience des nécessités de ton hygiène physique et intellectuelle. Fortifie-toi pour légitimer, chaque jour, tes dégoûts et tes mépris. ... [1]

Despite the tone and phrasing, much of which is taken directly from Barrès' own work,[2] it is not the style so much as the thought and attitude contained within these few sentences that is important—the same aloofness and the same egoism, a deliberate attempt by Mauriac to convince others and himself that he is superior to them. But this selection from Mauriac's notes is too brief to lead to any real appreciation of Barrès' influence, and it is in his first novel that the best commentary is found. Here too it is not only in the style but in the entire attitude to life developed by Jean-Paul that traces of Barrès are seen. At various points the scornful, cynical tone of the notes reproduced in *La Rencontre avec Barrès* is echoed: 'Ah! comme Jean-Paul les exécrait ces faces d'étudiants exténués, couverts de boutons, fendues par des rires.'[3] Vincent Hiéron also perceives this contempt in Jean-Paul: ' ... et quand on lisait certaines inepties, j'ai bien reconnu la façon dont s'abaissent les coins de ta bouche ... '.[4] In particular

[1] Ibid., pp. 182–3.
[2] Especially 'Ta fortune ... attitude' and 'vis au sommet ... barbares'. Cf. *Sous l'œil des barbares*, Paris, 1922, p. 207 and p. 236.
[3] *ECC*, O.C. t. x. 20.   [4] Ibid., p. 19.

it is Georges Élie the young worker who suffers most from Jean-Paul's superiority complex: 'Jean-Paul l'écoutait, un peu distrait, souriant parfois du savoureux accent local d'Élie'.[1] ' . . . il [Jean-Paul] trouvait un tel plaisir à éblouir cette petite âme obscure . . .'.[2]

In addition, we find the self-analysis so strongly advocated by Barrès in *Un Homme libre*: 'Au long d'une jeunesse isolée, calme, où il ne se passe rien, le jeune homme s'est habitué à se regarder lui-même vivre.'[3] But the real essence of the *barrésisme* of the novel lies not in passages like these, but in the movement and bearing of Jean-Paul through these few months of his life. It has already been suggested that the attraction which *Amour et foi* holds for Jean-Paul rests in the opportunity it affords him to display his personal abilities. Genuine piety or even religious fervour have no influence over his choice; it is entirely voluntary and deliberate. The same lack of genuine emotional participation enters his relationship with his cousin Marthe and with Louis Fauveau. At first he is content to enjoy Marthe's adoration, which he shows little inclination to return; he abandons both her and *Amour et foi* in an attempt to find satisfaction in the company of Fauveau, Liette and in the debauched life to which they introduce him. But all fails him. Jean-Paul's adventures in *L'Enfant chargé de chaînes* reflect Mauriac's own reactions to social, literary, emotional, or religious experience at this time in his life. Attention is drawn most directly to the last of these. Yet there is no mature, serious criticism of Social Catholicism in this novel. Although Mauriac has never been able—and indeed has never sought—to rid himself of the influence of Social Catholics, at this early stage in his career the whole affair was an adventure and Mauriac could not deceive himself in his sincerity for long. Sangnier had been right;[4] Mauriac was not of the stuff that militant *sillonistes* were made. For the moment Barrès and egoism spoke more appealingly than Sangnier and self-effacement.

---

[1] Ibid., p. 39. [2] Ibid., p. 40. [3] Ibid., p. 48.

[4] *NB-N*, p. 337. ' . . . il avait dû au premier regard discerner que je n'étais pas du bois dont on fait les militants. Les "intellectuels" n'avaient pas la cote au *Sillon*. Un petit barrésien de mon espèce était suspect avant d'avoir ouvert la bouche.' Cf. *MI*, p. 32, 'dans ce petit milieu du Sillon bordelais, j'apportais un esprit façonné par *Sous l'œil des barbares* et par *Un homme libre*.'

In many ways Jacques the young hero of Mauriac's second novel, *La Robe prétexte*, may be seen to represent the young man Jean-Paul Johanet was before he went to Paris. He shows the same enthusiasm for religious and romantic literature, enjoys the scent-laden summers of the landes and shares an innocent first love affair with his cousin Camille. But here the similarity ends. On the whole this novel shows slightly less certainty in its composition than the first, in which Jean-Paul's association with *Amour et Foi* not only reflects Mauriac's own experiences, but provides some form of focal point in an otherwise rather incoherent pattern.

When *La Robe prétexte* was included in the first volume of his *Œuvres complètes*, Mauriac rejected it in much the same way that he rejected the effusive piety of *Les Mains jointes* in 1927: 'La mollesse de ce style, l'influence, pour ne pas dire l'imitation du Jammes de *Clara d'Ellébeuse*, bien d'autres défauts me le rendent aujourd'hui assez odieux.'[1] The similarity of detail with Jammes' novel, however, is only superficial: Jacques' father's flight to Tahiti in some ways echoes Clara's uncle Joachim's exotic journeys and in particular his stay in Guadeloupe where he met the unfortunate Laura; Jacques and Camille both show certain characteristics of Clara herself, while Philippe Ducasse's arrival from Paris is clearly patterned on Roger Fauchereuse's visit in Jammes' novel. Moreover, the simple, sentimental tone of the earlier work is recreated by Mauriac though he fortunately avoids the temptation to depict any character as naïve as Clara herself, who believes that 'c'est par des *embrassements* que naissent les enfants'.[2]

Jacques' life is dominated on the one hand by religion personified by the trio of pious women who are responsible for his upbringing, and on the other by his own 'goût du romanesque'.[3] For the most part the former is the more influential: discovering that his rosary is no longer around his wrist when he wakes in the morning, his first thought is that he has committed 'un sacrilège innocent',[4] confession is 'le plus délicat plaisir',[5] he enjoys participating in

---

[1] O.C. t. i. *Préface*, p. I.
[2] *Clara d'Ellébeuse*, Œuvres de Francis Jammes, Vol. III, Paris, 1923, p. 88.
[3] *RP*, O.C. t. i. 6.   [4] Ibid., p. 4.   [5] Ibid., p. 102.

religious ceremonies,[1] favourable examination results depend on
God's approval and not the examiners',[2] and his adolescent love
for Camille is blessed by the Virgin Mary.[3] Within this protective
shell, however, the attractions of the outer world are already
beginning to have their effect. Jacques is fascinated by his free
living and free thinking uncle, always in pursuit of 'des voluptés
inconnues'. He rapidly learns the ways of Parisian life and his
quick conquest of Liette is proof enough of his taste for this easy
career, even if his desire is for the moment tinged with remorse.[4]
More significantly of course Jacques is haunted by the memory of
his dead father, whose search for freedom and light had led him
away from the claustrophobia of Ousilanne, his young wife, and
the cloying influence of religious observation.

La Robe prétexte, as the title suggests, is the story of a coming of
age as Jacques leaves behind his childhood with its particular
beauty and innocent pleasures, and emerges into an adult world.
But this change could not be made without pain or sacrifice.
José Ximenès, Jacques' strange Spanish classmate (who is to
reappear as Augustin in Préséances), had sought to preserve the
mystery of youth but had only done so at the expense of death.
Jacques lives on into a twilight autumnal world[5] where Ousilanne
is to be sold and where Camille has changed from the carefree
girl he had loved as a boy into a young woman who is now
'indifférente et affairée'[6] and who is resigned to the prospect of
marrying 'un homme fait, un esprit pratique'.[7] Jacques' only
consolation lies in his faith that he and Camille will be eternally
reunited in death.

Taken together, L'Enfant chargé de chaînes and La Robe prétexte
show many similarities in style and composition: both are heavily
weighted with exaggerated autobiographical detail, they reflect
Mauriac's own tastes in literature at this time, and above all tend
to be diffuse and uncontrolled. Such features continue to be found
in Mauriac's next two novels, La Chair et le sang begun in 1914
but not finished and published until six years later, and Préséances
(1921). There can be little doubt that the intended continuity of

[1] Ibid., p. 14. [2] Ibid., p. 78. [3] Ibid., p. 96.
[4] Ibid., pp. 125–6. [5] Ibid., p. 144. [6] Ibid., p. 130.
[7] Ibid., p. 136.

La Chair et le sang was damaged by the enforced interruption of the war years, yet there are also undeniable signs that Mauriac's ambitions were still in excess of his skill as a novelist. From the title it would appear that the novel should have centred on the spiritual conflict of Claude Favereau: '[. . .] il eût pu, lui aussi, devenir un saint, mais la chair et le sang l'avaient asservi . . . '.[1] Yet while he may have been unsuited for the bookish atmosphere of the seminary, Claude's spiritual purity is never in doubt. Mauriac emphasizes his participation and enjoyment in the natural world around him: 'Lui, il ne veut pas dormir, mais s'abandonner âme et corps à cette chaleur qui perd sa vie dans la Vie.'[2] His total absorption into the peasant world to which he belongs nullifies any carnal thoughts he has concerning May and thereby is given an extra dimension:

Cette animalité le sauvait. Cette matière pétrie par lui, avec laquelle il lui semblait se confondre, l'arrachait aux obsédantes pensées; l'ancien lévite, délivré de la tentation par un excès de fatigue, en remerciait Dieu chaque soir dans le soupir de fatigue et de foi qui lui servait de prière.[3]

But Claude's spiritual crises and his willingness to assume total responsibility for Edward's sins[4] are too easily lost behind the whole range of personal relationships that are scattered throughout this novel. Edith Gonzalès, for example, remains for much of the time apart in her world of social and literary pretentions, Edward, who could be seen on occasions as the principal character, conceals his sense of solitude and emptiness behind a mask of boredom and cynicism, while May's marriage and conversion assumes its own significance independent of Claude. In the tradition of *L'Enfant chargé de chaînes* and *La Robe prétexte*, *La Chair et le sang* is basically a collection of sub-plots and only occasionally, by the use of a letter or May's journal, is Mauriac able to connect them with any degree of success.

In spite of this diffuse nature, however, certain features of *La Chair et le sang* already indicate major themes of Mauriac's subsequent work. The satirical depiction of the bourgeois world,

[1] *CS*, O.C. t. x. 252–3.   [2] Ibid., p. 145.   [3] Ibid., p. 246.
[4] Ibid., pp. 165–6.

for example, has been so sharpened that it bears little resemblance
to the insipid observations on sentimental piety made in *La Robe
prétexte*, and already as we shall notice in Chapter Four, Mauriac's
stylistic techniques are beginning to take shape. More important
is the deliberate introduction of Grace, and *La Chair et le sang* may
be said to be Mauriac's first attempt at writing a Catholic novel,
in other words a novel in which Catholicism does not simply
create a certain atmosphere or even become materialized in the
form of a religious programme or movement, such as *Amour et foi*,
but in which it plays an active part and influences the lives of
those persons who are attracted to it. For May marriage to Marcel
Castagnède necessitates conversion from Protestantism, the faith
which she and Edward have been brought up to accept. Mauriac
is at pains to demonstrate that Edward's increasing sense of
solitude, his father's fear of death and May's feeling of guilt after
she has kissed Claude ('[. . .] comme sa religion la laissait seule'[1])
are all the result of their Protestantism. But the marriage is a formal
excuse only. Already her conversations with Claude have
indicated to May the insufficiency of her religion and the need
instead for her to be able to communicate directly with God
through prayer and confession. Mauriac uses the device of the
private journal to show what effect conversion to Catholicism
has on May: 'Sentiment, certitude désormais d'un refuge contre
toute la vie. Plus jamais seule.'[2] Her new faith is unshakeable and
brilliantly exposes the paucity of her brother's existence and, by
implication, that of all Protestants. But as an event her conversion
does not dominate the novel[3], and whether or not it is convincing
hardly seems relevant. None the less Mauriac had made a first
attempt at incorporating Catholicism as a living force in his
imaginative writing, though it is not for another ten years that
the idea of conversion assumes central importance and obliges
Mauriac to adapt his technique accordingly. Until then Mauriac's
talent develops in other directions, particularly in his exposure of
the valueless existence led by the bourgeois world of Bordeaux

[1] Ibid., p. 182.   [2] Ibid., p. 214.
[3] An interesting case could be made out for the christo-pagan symbolism of
the month of May and the relationship between rebirth and conversion which is of
central importance in later novels. See below, Chapter Four.

and the *landes*. This is not to say that religion is totally absent from his work, but as is suggested by Gide's criticism it can only be there by implication and his predilections clearly lie elsewhere. *Préséances*, the last of these early, experimental novels, satirizes bourgeois society in an unnecessarily exaggerated fashion, as Mauriac confessed in 1928, though at the same time the appearance of Augustin represents the link with the religious romanticism evident in the first three novels.

This work traces the movements of the anonymous narrator's family within the fashionable society of Bordeaux. Florence his sister, like Edith Gonzalès in *La Chair et le sang*, is particularly aware of the social advantages to be won if she can marry one of the 'Fils', the heirs to the fortunes amassed from the long and careful cultivation of vines. While awaiting her opportunity Florence flirts selfishly and cruelly with Augustin who is in her brother's class. Augustin, who is illegitimate and like Rimbaud on whom he is clearly figured[1] despises the trivialities of this society's existence, eventually departs for Sénégal. Even after the disillusioning effect of meeting him again, when both he and Florence are considerably older, he remains a symbol of true values against which all social pretentions and superficiality are to be judged. Once again the novel fails because Mauriac's principal intention is never very obvious. Clearly the book is intended as a satire but considerable weight is also given to the mental anguish of the narrator who has introduced Augustin to this worthless society, and also to Florence's inability to escape the demands of lust which make her a forerunner of Gisèle de Plailly in *Le Fleuve de feu*.

Mauriac's main target for satire is the assumed superiority of those whose fortunes have been made from the vineyards and who despise the more recently acquired wealth of the pine forest magnates. The narrator's family belongs to this second society, yet it is soon made clear that its main aim in life is to emulate the society which in turn it claims to despise. His family can never maintain the complete detachment shown by Augustin, and when the chance for their son to share some of the social glory normally reserved for the 'Fils' arises, all other matters are put aside:

[1] O.C. t. x. *Préface*, p. III.

THE FIRST STEPS 47

Ma famille vécut des semaines dans le tremblement; ne serais-je pas
mis à l'écart d'un rallye où seul figurait le dessus du panier? il y eut
des conciliabules à mon sujet: le fils Harry Maucoudinat, chef d'une
faction puissante, ne pensait pas que le fils d'un marchand de bois pût
jamais paraître sur un mail-coach. Mon oncle sauva une cause qui
paraissait perdue, en répandant le bruit que je possédais un habit rouge
(au vrai nous n'en fîmes la commande que lorsqu'il fut avéré qu'à cet
habit je devrais figurer en haut du mail-coach, parmi les Fils des
grandes Maisons et tout baigné de leur gloire, au point que l'on pourrait
me prendre pour l'un d'eux!)[1]

Similarly both types of society are guilty of an anglomania
reflected in their speech, dress and even 'le bureau de leur cercle
London et Westminster[2] which they believe is a mark of culture
and superiority. The worthlessness of all such social pretention,
from which only Augustin escapes, is finally recorded at the
uncle's funeral. That his life-long struggle for social respectability
has been vindicated is evident from the 'deux cent vingt-sept
chapeaux de soie du cercle de *London et Westminster*' which
attend the body. As Florence sarcastically remarks: 'Quel dom-
mage [...] que le bon homme ne soit plus là pour les voir et
pour les compter!'[3]

In spite of their differences, each of these four early works
shows Mauriac (perhaps unconsciously) exploring various forms
of the Catholic novel. In *L'Enfant chargé de chaînes* only the
autobiographical element prevents his brief excursion into the
politico-religious world of the *Sillon* becoming a piece of semi-
documentary writing rather in the manner of *Les Saints vont en
enfer*; in *La Robe prétexte* he draws on and exaggerates the religious
atmosphere of his early years; in *La Chair et le sang* we find
Catholicism compared unfavourably with Protestantism together
with the first signs of the natural and seasonal pattern that
Mauriac was to develop to such advantage in later works. Only
Préséances may be said to stand a little to one side of the others,
but even in this novel the presence of Augustin and the implied
criticism of the importance given to material values looks forward
to the indirect approval of Catholicism which underlies the
portrayal of Mauriac's bourgeois world.

[1] *P*, O.C. t. x. 283.   [2] Ibid., p. 294.   [3] Ibid., p. 341.

Already the essential ingredients of Mauriac's work had made their appearance—the bitter, pessimistic depiction of bourgeois society on the one hand and the natural and animal world on the other. Together they form a pattern that dominates his subsequent work and which is eventually fashioned to contain the successful Catholic novel.

3

MAURIAC'S BOURGEOIS WORLD

Ils ont l'air de courir après la fortune, mais ce n'est pas après la fortune qu'ils
courent: c'est eux-mêmes qu'ils fuient.   GEORGES BERNANOS

LIKE Pascal, his spiritual guide for so many years, Mauriac
depicts in his novels the 'misère de l'homme sans Dieu',
and a world which, obsessed with the need for immediate
material benefit, is unwilling to place its faith in spiritual values
and the possibility of ultimate salvation. Unlike Pascal, however,
he is reluctant to make a general open statement about mankind,
for as a novelist his aim is to convince not by rational argument
but by illustration. From the very first novels, the south-west of
France—offset by an occasional excursion to Paris—features
prominently, insulated from the outside world, hemmed in and
controlled by certain standards and requirements which ensure
its continuing prosperity.

In *L'Enfant chargé de chaînes* Jean-Paul and his cousin Marthe
are both natives of the *landes* where their fathers pass the time
between the pleasures of hunting and the problem of buying
and selling pines to the best advantage. Even so the main develop-
ments of the book take place in Paris, a feature readopted in two
later novels only—*Ce qui était perdu* and *La Fin de la nuit*. Yet
even in these the link with Bordeaux and the *landes* is never
entirely lost. In the first the arrival of Alain Forcas refreshes his
sister's desire to leave her husband and Paris: in the second the
action ultimately reverts to the *landes* with the return home of
Thérèse, broken in spirit. In *Le Désert de l'amour* Raymond
Courrèges 'narrates' the story from a Parisian bar, though the
actual subject matter deals with his home life and adolescence in
Bordeaux. In the rest of the novels many of Mauriac's characters
make excursions of varying lengths to the capital: Edward in
La Chair et le sang, Jacques in *La Robe prétexte*, Jean Péloueyre in
Le Baiser au lépreux, Fabien in *Le Mal* and Yves Frontenac in *Le*

Mystère Frontenac for example. Nevertheless as in *Ce qui était perdu* the temporary exile is always surrounded by a feeling of unrest, a feeling that serves Mauriac's purpose in pointing to the superficiality and shifting nature of life there. The only novel in which the drama takes place outside these two main centres is *Le Fleuve de feu* in which Daniel Trassis and Gisèle de Plailly satisfy their passions in a second rate hotel in the Pyrenees, yet even in this novel references are continually made to the *landes*, Daniel's native region, and to Paris, his customary haunt, as though Mauriac did not wish—or could not avoid—that this one book should be an exception.

If by 'provincial' we are to understand an inability or refusal to depict any region but one's own, Mauriac would certainly feature prominently on any list of provincial novelists. He has written not a series of individual separate novels but a body of work in which we find recurrent features. In addition to the usually sparse, direct descriptions of pine forests, vineyards, and rambling country houses, he attempts to give the impression of a closely inter-related society by the obvious but fairly effective device of a cross reference system of names. Not only are the characters of one novel mentioned in another simply as relations, acquaintances, or neighbours, but occasionally they reappear to play a considerable part in the action. Thus the Cazenave family appears as a threat to the heritage of the Péloueyre in *Le Baiser au lépreux* only to be recalled by the author a year later to form the nucleus of another novel, *Génitrix*. In two pairs of novels in particular, *Thérèse Desqueyroux* and *La Fin de la nuit*, *La Pharisienne* and *L'Agneau*, the reappearance of characters suggests that the novels are sequels even though this is specifically denied by Mauriac: 'Il n'est aucunement nécessaire d'avoir connu la première Thérèse pour s'intéresser à celle dont je raconte ici le dernier amour.'[1] Similarly in *L'Agneau* he writes: 'Les lecteurs de *la Pharisienne* retrouveront ici Jean de Mirbel, Michèle et Brigitte Pian. Non qu'il s'agisse d'une suite ou d'un épilogue: la tragédie de *L'Agneau* n'est liée en rien à l'histoire que je racontais il y a quinze ans.'[2] While this may be true even for the first pair of novels, it does not alter the fact that such recurrence binds his

[1] *FN*, p. 5.   [2] Op. cit., p. 5.

work together, though as a novelistic device this feature hardly bears comparison with the intricate ramifications of Balzac's society in *La Comédie humaine*.

Enveloping this picture of *bordelais* society and nourishing its intrigues and passions we find the typical furnace summers and mist-laden winters of that region. These two seasons of extremes dominate, and human moods are equally violent; as Mauriac writes in *Génitrix*: 'les passions des hommes s'accordent à la violence du ciel'.[1] Such interdependence of mood and weather can be multiplied from novel to novel, as can the identification of man with the pine trees and vines. Mauriac elaborates on what he has experienced himself and what he saw around him as a boy. It is impossible to separate man from his environment; he has been born into it and has no choice; escape is impossible and even if, like Mauriac himself, he is able to withdraw physically, he retains the indelible stamp of his provincial upbringing.

In the second volume of his *Journal* Mauriac describes how Edouard Bourdet once suggested to him that he should remove the unsightly slates put on part of the roof at Malagar by his grandfather. Mauriac's answer is at once immediate and significant: 'Enlever les ardoises? Je n'ai pas envie que mes paysans me prennent pour un fou!'[2] The feeling he has that it would be unwise to provoke his peasant workers in this way indicates how aware he is that the peasants and the bourgeoisie of the *landes* are basically of the same stock, joined in a common worship of the land: 'le goût commun de la terre, de la chasse, du manger et du boire, crée entre tous, bourgeois et paysans, une fraternité étroite'.[3] Careful, hostile to change, and astute the peasants can only be differentiated from their bourgeois neighbours by their lack of wealth and social prestige: each of these classes in fact could be

cette sainte classe moyenne, soucieuse de ne dédaigner aucune promesse, de ne courir aucun risque inutile, fût-il d'ordre métaphysique; race prudente, circonspecte, sage, dont toutes les polices d'assurance sont en règle pour le temps et pour l'éternité.[4]

---

[1] Op. cit., O.C. t. i. 374.   [2] Op. cit., p. 10.
[3] *TD*, p. 84.   [4] *B*, O.C. t. iv. 167.

Dominique Favereau in *La Chair et le sang*, for example, typifies the peasant's attitude to life in general when he scorns scientific recommendations for the tending of his vines:

—Le journal dit qu'il faut soufrer la vigne sur la fleur. Moi j'ai déjà fait un soufrage avant.

Il avait en lui-même une foi absolue et pour les 'savants' un infini mépris. Il exigeait d'être écouté comme un oracle, et sa femme, depuis trente ans approuvait les sentences que le bonhomme rendait d'un air profond: le phylloxéra n'avait jamais existé, c'était une invention des savants, il était plein de telles certitudes.[1]

Similar caution dogs any monetary transactions. Robert, Louis' bastard son in *Le Nœud de vipères*, is unwilling to accept his father's word that there will be no repercussions on the money he is to inherit: 'Ce qui demeurait puissant chez ce calicot, c'était l'instinct paysan de prévoyance, l'horreur du risque, le souci de ne rien laisser au hasard.'[2] So cautious and withdrawn are these peasants that even the young priest in *Le Sagouin* cannot understand them, and finds that his Christian charity withers before their refusal to communicate with him: 'Une espèce de haine lui était venue contre cette humanité paysanne, imperméable à qui il ne savait pas parler, occupée uniquement de la terre et qui n'avait besoin de lui.'[3]

This vigorous provincialism from which it seems that Mauriac, like his characters, is unable to escape has led not unnaturally to considerable criticism of his work. Heppenstall, for example, objects that it falsifies Mauriac's presentation of moral problems,[4] Clouard that it presents the reader with 'une lassante uniformité',[5] yet not only does Mauriac believe in the retention of his native environment as one of the essential elements of his fictional writing, we also see it as a means which enables him to concentrate on the projection of certain views and opinions into his work without having to give unnecessary attention to the more usual trappings of setting and atmosphere.

Such provincial isolation is paralleled by one in time. In essence

---

[1] Op. cit., O.C. t. x. 249.   [2] Op. cit., p. 163.   [3] Op. cit., p. 29.
[4] *The Double Image*, London, 1947, p. 46.
[5] *Histoire de la littérature française du symbolisme à nos jours*, Vol. II, Paris, 1949, p. 278.

all of Mauriac's novels belong to the last years of the nineteenth and the first two decades or so of the twentieth centuries. His depiction of Bordeaux and the *landes* is based on a recollection of the period of his childhood and adolescence; that of Paris primarily on his life there after the First World War. While some novels such as *La Chair et le sang* and *La Pharisienne* do contain precise indications of the year in which the action is meant to occur, it is generally from incidental material that such information is to be gleaned. Like most of the financially successful families from around Bordeaux, Mauriac's own owed its wealth to a considerable holding of vineyards and pine forests. Fortunes had been prepared or even made in the nineteenth century through careful agricultural planning, balancing one product against another in times of disease and extensive fires. The planting of the vast pine estates was of particular importance since not only did land hitherto impossible to cultivate now assume immense value, but losses incurred by the ravages of phylloxera between 1860 and the turn of the century could on many occasions be almost entirely offset. Mauriac's family was no exception in its astute, professional approach to the management of its estates, and in *Les Maisons fugitives* he quotes the formula which, when backed by natural and material resources, could not fail to lead to prosperity:

De l'arrière-grand-père mort sous l'Empire, celui qui vers 1840 acheta Malagar, je sais qu'il était fort sentencieux et développait volontiers les trois points du même discours: ordre, travail, économie. Je suis né au plus beau moment de la troisième période, lorsque la fourmi entasse. Mettre de côté, placer, accroître le capital: 'Vous me remercierez plus tard . . .' et autour du trésor, la garde montée, la mobilisation de l'instinct conservateur.[1]

Such progressive accumulation and thrifty management of wealth are reflected in the novels. Elisabeth Gornac's father, Hector Lavignasse in *Destins*, overcomes the financial losses incurred through disease by investment in pines: 'ruiné par le phylloxéra, [il] avait refait sa fortune grâce à une usine de térébenthine . . .'.[2] Hourtinat in *Préséances* is another who has

---

[1] Op. cit., t. iv. 323. [2] Op. cit., O.C. t. i. 432.

prospered in the same way, and Jean-Paul Johanet's father and uncle can look forward to a comfortable old age 'surtout que le bois, aujourd'hui, vaut tant d'argent'.[1] Wine, the more traditional product of the region, also features prominently. *Destins* in particular recalls the occasional exceptional harvests which appeared during the period largely dominated by disease and which seemed to compensate for its overall failure. Yet wealth, however achieved, brings no attendant material extravagance, especially for those families living in the decaying mansions of the *landes*, and even in Bordeaux itself where families tend, as in *Le Rang* or *Préséances*, to be more ostentatious and conscious of their social position, the cautious, almost miserly, attitude of the peasants remains very evident. Money is simply a means by which they can make more. Fernand Cazenave is content to allow his pines to work on his behalf: 'il connut comme il est facile d'avoir dans une banque un compte ouvert, et que les pins poussent tout seuls'.[2] Louis in *Le Nœud de vipères* on the other hand accelerates the process through the buying and selling of shares. But whichever way is adopted the result is the same. Mauriac's novels reflect a period of material prosperity; it was not difficult, it seems, to be in the position of Armand Dubernet who in *Galigaï* 'avait de quoi vivre sans travailler'.[3]

In comparison Mauriac's few treatments of Paris are hardly more flattering. In spite of his many years there, the capital has remained for Mauriac very much the large, impersonal city it had appeared to him as a young man. Jacques and his family in *La Robe prétexte* feel honoured by the visit of Philippe Ducasse simply because he lives there: 'cela seul lui donnait à nos yeux un étonnant prestige'.[4] But this impression is exploded once Jacques has tasted Parisian life for himself. For nearly all the provincial characters in Mauriac's novels Paris has only empty and fleeting pleasures to offer, and existence there results in the obliteration of all individuality. The Parisian is a type in his own right who imposes his peculiar characteristics on all who are not strong enough to resist them. If he offers no resistance the impotent provincial is slowly assimilated to the Parisian way of life, until he is eventually

[1] *ECC*, O.C. t. x. 83.   [2] *G*, O.C. t. i. 387.
[3] Op. cit., p. 7.   [4] Op. cit., O.C. t. i. 82.

stamped with the common brand of anonymity: 'Paris nous impose un uniforme; il nous met, comme ses maisons, à l'alignement; il estrompe les caractères, nous réduit à un type commun.'[1] It is to such anonymity that Larousselle objects in *Le Désert de l'amour*: 'ce que Larousselle ne pouvait souffrir à Paris, c'était le nombre infini des têtes qu'il n'y connaissait pas. Dans sa ville il n'était guère de figures qui ne lui rappelassent un nom, des alliances et qu'il ne pût situer d'un coup d'œil, soit à sa droite parmi les gens auxquels on montre de la courtoisie, soit à sa gauche avec les réprouvés qu'on connaît, mais qu'on ne salue pas.'[2] Larousselle's uneasiness and irritation is echoed in Alain Forcas' physical incapacity to endure the stifling atmosphere of a night club,[3] and even his sister Tota, whose nymphomaniac inclinations would seem suited to Parisian life, is hallmarked as a provincial: 'la petite provinciale ne savait pas encore traverser les rues'.[4] Paris is guilty of encouraging both immorality and instability; of having fostered jazz and 'la peste noire surréaliste',[5] escapist cults which according to Mauriac have relieved the younger generation in particular of any need to indulge in self-analysis or introspection: 'Tout est bon selon eux, qui suspend la réflexion, la pensée, qui les détourne de se voir eux-mêmes et de voir les autres.'[6]

At the same time Mauriac is equally ready to criticize his own society's peculiarly narrow and refracted vision of life, and in particular its readiness to erect material values above spiritual ones. Motivated by money and material possession it stifles all forms of individualism. For some—Augustin, Maryan or even Gabriel Gradère—its problems are apparently the petty quarrels of an enclosed rural community. Jealousy, avarice, ambition, love, and hate are worked out with nature as an accomplice and contained by the 'barrages de la religion, par les hiérarchies sociales',[7] with a consequent increase in pitch. Even Thérèse Desqueyroux cannot remain uninfluenced by the value her society places in property, and however unwilling she may be

---

[1] *PR*, O.C. t. iv. 458.   [2] Op. cit., pp. 210–11.
[3] *CP*, O.C. t. iii. 51.   [4] Ibid., p. 73.
[5] *J*, II. 159.   [6] *J, I*, O.C. t. xi. 11.
[7] *PR*, O.C. t. iv. 457.

she has no choice but to be aware of the value of her husband's estates: 'Les deux mille hectares de Bernard ne l'avaient pas laissé indifférente. "Elle avait toujours eu la propriété dans le sang." '[1] Such wealth represented by acres of pine-forests or vineyards leads on to the most dominating idol of all, social rank: 'L'intelligence, ni l'esprit, ni le talent n'entrent en ligne de compte, mais seulement la position.'[2]

A social pattern based on the worship of money with its attendant social prestige evolves and holds Mauriac's families in a firm grip. Blind and implicit obedience to the cult renders them powerless to adapt themselves to events which are in any way unusual. Trivialities are wildly exaggerated. Bernard Desqueyroux, for example, the prosperous and successful owner of thousands of pine trees, is thrown into spasms of anxiety by the discrepancy between timetables at the railway stations and those in Baedeker. Like Fernand Cazenave his mind is 'moins exercée aux idées qu'aux chiffres'[3] and it is impossible for him to possess the same curiosity and interest in matters outside the administration of his estates as does his wife. His world consists of his family, which like all of Mauriac's bourgeois families is a microscopic exaggeration of the society to which they belong. Features are enlarged almost to the point of distortion with Mauriac presenting us in most cases with the final stages in a long process of disintegration and decay.

It is the fear not so much of death as of the possibility of losing wealth, and hence prestige in the eyes of others, that dictates families' attitudes. Each recognizes the need to guard its holdings jealously and to supplement them at every opportunity:

Ils ne doutaient pas que le domaine, après eux, dût passer à leurs enfants et à leurs petits enfants. 'Quoiqu'il arrive, ne vendez jamais la terre.' Ce fut toujours une de leurs dernières paroles. On s'arrangeait pour ne pas la vendre et pour que les propriétés d'un seul tenant gardassent leur unité. Depuis la Révolution, il y eut toujours, par génération, un oncle célibataire, dont la part revenait aux neveux, afin que l'héritage, à peine divisé, se reformât.[4]

Death is regarded as little more than a relatively insignificant

[1] TD, p. 42.   [2] PR, O.C. t. iv. 457.   [3] G, O.C. t. i. 327.
[4] J, I, O.C. t. xi. 20.

interruption of what is above all a commercial process; any threat to the progress of this is seen as 'le mal absolu'[1] to be fought at all costs.

In the same way as social prestige accentuates rivalries between families and stifles all attempts at individual expression, so too do the narrow precincts of the family circle make the various pressures to conform more acute. The enclosed aspect of the *landes* country house is as authentic for the rebel who seeks to escape as it is for the outsider who ponders over its impassive appearance.[2] Physical and mental imprisonment may be symbolized, as in *Thérèse Desqueyroux* for example, by the encircling pines, or expressed in the family hostility felt by Paul Courrèges in *Le Désert de l'amour*. Noémi Péloueyre, bound for commercial reasons to eternal widowhood, realizes too late the horror of her predicament: 'Elle éprouvait que les pins innombrables, aux entrailles rouges et gluantes, que les sables et les landes incendiées la garderaient à jamais prisonnière.'[3] Thérèse Desqueyroux, the person most embittered by the restrictions forced upon her by her husband's family, typifies a whole attitude of revolt: 'La famille. Thérèse laissa éteindre sa cigarette; l'œil fixe, elle regardait cette cage aux barreaux innombrables et vivants, cette cage tapissé d'oreilles et d'yeux, où, immobile, accroupie le menton aux genoux, les bras entourants ses jambes, elle attendait de mourir.'[4] For people like Thérèse or Paule Meulière in *Le Sagouin* the plight is all the more distressing because they have sought happiness or at least security as they think quite rationally, trusting that in marriage and family life their individual demands will be satisfied, and only when it is too late to turn back do they realize that the opposite is true. As one who, through her marriage to Galéas de Cernès, has managed to penetrate beyond the traditional barriers of class prejudice, Paule discovers that the life she once believed so inaccessible now encompasses her so firmly

[1] *NMI*, p. 126.
[2] G, O.C. t. i. 376. 'Mais rien n'est moins accessible aux regards, ni plus propice au mystère que ces domaines ceints de murs et enserrés si étroitement d'arbres, qu'il semble que les êtres qui vivent là n'aient aucune autre communication qu'entre eux ou avec le ciel.'
[3] *BL*, O.C. t. i. 211–12.
[4] *TD*, pp. 60–1. Cf. *DA*, pp. 119–20; *NV*, p. 90.

that she finds it impossible to escape: 'Elle n'ignore plus aujourd'
hui que ce qu'on appelle un milieu fermé, l'est à la lettre: y
pénétrer semblait difficile, presque impossible; mais en sortir! . . . '¹
To an onlooker such bitterness remains hidden and the family
continues to present its impassive appearance to the outside
world: 'La famille oppose à l'étranger un bloc sans fissures; mais
à l'intérieur, que de rivalités furieuses.'² Even Gabriel Gradère in
Les Anges noirs soon finds himself involved in the Desbats family's
plots and counterplots as he struggles to free himself from Aline's
blackmailing grasp.

Mauriac's families are not bound together by love, but by a
sense of possession, a deep-rooted mania for holding their
properties at all costs. In *La Robe prétexte* relations carefully check
their numbers at the end of every year to ensure that they are
still at full strength to continue their struggle for existence. All is
planned in terms of the future, and only carefree children can
temporarily afford to enjoy life.³ As Hélène Guénot so rightly
observed: 'Ce n'est pas un lien spirituel qui les [les membres de la
famille] attache ensemble, mais l'instinct de conservation sous
toutes ses formes qui les plie à sa loi.'⁴ Inevitably the nature of
marriage suffers. Convenience is the only sure method of con-
serving and at best of increasing existing fortunes. For here is a
society in which a daughter's dowry could not only drastically
reduce a family's wealth temporarily but could be lost for ever.
This is the problem which obsesses Symphorien Desbats in *Les
Anges noirs* and which he only solves after a series of carefully
balanced commercial manœuvres by which he is able to ensure that
during his life he will remain the sole head of the family estates,
and that after his death they will pass to Andrès as his only heir.
In *Le Baiser au lépreux* Jean's marriage to Noémi d'Artiailh is an
attempt to prevent the wealth moving out of the direct line of
descent to his cousin and only other possible male successor,
Fernand Cazenave. As a physical marriage, however, the match is
a failure and it is noticeable that throughout the book we should
continue to think of Noémi by her maiden name and not as Mme

¹ S, p. 6.   ² PR, O.C. t. iv. 459.
³ Op. cit., O.C. t. i. 29.
⁴ *Nouvelles littéraires*, 25 October 1930, p. 9.

Péloueyre, an impression that is reinforced by the particular imagery used by Mauriac in describing their relationship.[1] Noémi and Jean have been brought together in an attempt to solve a commercial problem which is not their immediate concern. Noémi in particular is no more than a puppet, powerless to prevent her parents and the priest from directing her life and taking her decisions for her, yet so perfectly formed is her sense of social requirement that it never occurs to her to object:

Les parents de Noémi, s'ils vivent dans l'angoisse que le jeune homme se dérobe, n'imaginent même pas qu'aucune objection vienne de leur fille; elle n'y songe pas non plus.[2]

Such submission is shared by the majority of the daughters in Mauriac's bourgeois families and accompanies them beyond marriage into their own adult lives, when their sole duty becomes that of producing an heir to the family estate. This life of willing self-sacrifice ages them all prematurely. As Jacques discovers in La Robe prétexte on his return to Ousilanne, Camille has become a woman both physically and mentally, and Elisabeth Gornac's confessor is right when he remarks: 'Vous êtes bien toutes les mêmes, ma pauvre fille ... quand on connaît l'une de vous, on connaît toutes.'[3] Even such notable exceptions to the pattern as Thérèse Desqueyroux or Maria Cross, branded by their community as intellectuals, can only writhe uncomfortably for a while before finally succumbing to pressures which are too strong for them.

While such submission may earn society's approval it can never entirely gloss over the disharmony that prevails at the heart of the family. Frustration and irritation gradually erode all human relationships and in particular that between a mother and the son she has been required to bear. This is most fully worked out in Le Baiser au lépreux and Génitrix. In the former Félicité Cazenave's hostility to Fernand's prospects of marriage is quite open: 'On racontait qu'elle avait dit un jour: "Si Fernand se marie, ma bru mourra."'[4] Mathilde does to be sure temporarily draw her

[1] See below, Chapter Four, p. 70.   [2] BL, O.C. t. i. 165.
[3] D, O.C. t. i. 532.   [4] Op. cit., O.C. t. i. 158.

husband away from Félicité's influence, from 'ce réseau [...]
cette toile gluante',[1] but her mother-in-law's threats soon
materialize for within two months Fernand has left the marriage
bed and returned to 'son petit lit de collégien tout contre la
chambre maternelle',[2] and Mathilde dies from neglect. Ironically
Mathilde's most substantial success in possessing her husband's
mind—so substantial that in turn Félicité dies—occurs after her
own death, though the mother eventually wins this battle of wills
when her spirit is reincarnated in her son.[3] Perfect though it may
be, Mauriac's treatment of this particular theme in this early pair
of novels is by its extreme nature exceptional, and in general it is
the mother who suffers for her obstinate attempts to preserve the
mythology of childhood in her adolescent and even adult son.[4]
On the other hand, however, absolute escape for the child is
equally impossible; the result is a vicious circle: 'A mesure qu'il
grandit, l'enfant-tyran devient lui-même peu à peu l'esclave de
sa mère esclave; il ne peut plus se passer de sa victime; il la
tourmente, mais il lui est asservi.'[5]

It is of course doubly ironical that the need to procreate should
not only result in this type of love-hate duel between mother and
child, but should also debase the marital relationships of the
parents. Intimacy usually only lasts long enough for one child
to be produced before the couple decide to 'faire chambre à part'.[6]
Frequently sexual relationships are overlain with actual physical
loathing nowhere better exemplified than by the single-paged
icy Chapter Five in Le Baiser au lépreux which describes Jean and
Noémi's wedding night.[7] Men either show ignorance[8] or physical
incompetence before their marriage bed,[9] while women appear

---

[1] G, O.C. t. i. 368.   [2] Ibid., O.C. t. i. 328.

[3] Ibid., O.C. t. i. 399. 'Et il rejetait sa tête, le cou gonflé comme une Junon,—et
l'on eût dit sa mère vivante.'

[4] See for example Mme Dézaymeries and Fabien in M; Mme de Blaye and Jean
in PL (Conte de Noël); Mme Plassac and Nicolas in GAL.   [5] EF, p. 177.

[6] See, for example G, TD, AN, S. It is noticeable that even in MF the happiness
of the marriage shared by Blanche and Michel is always referred to in retrospect.

[7] O.C. t. i. 171.

[8] Numa Cazenave in G for example. O.C. t. i. 365. 'Au moment de prendre
femme, il dut demander à un ami comment on se sert d'une femme.'

[9] Symphorien Desbats in AN, p. 140, and Jean de Mirbel's impotence in A. See
below, Chapter Six, p. 101.

to have an innate fear reminiscent of the Bossuet which Mauriac edited in 1927, seeming to consider sexual relations as a sure step towards damnation.[1] Most of them shrink before the slightest approach from their husband and even Thérèse accepts Bernard only to provide herself with an exercise in deception.[2]

Mental and physical incompatibility of this kind is emphasized and worsened when we consider the narrow segment of society from which the majority of these couples come. Mauriac writes in *La Province* that 'Beaucoup de jeunes filles, en Province, se marient dans leur ville et, s'il est possible, dans leur quartier,'[3] and the resultant inbreeding is in turn reflected in the novels. Elisabeth Gornac in *Destins* amusingly explains to Bob Lagave how she and Paule de la Sesque are related:

> Mais sa mère et moi, nous nous appelons par nos prénoms. D'ailleurs nous sommes cousins. . . . Je ne saurais très bien vous dire comment. . . . Au fait, si . . . et même cousins assez rapprochés: l'arrière-grand-mère de la petite était la demi-sœur de mon grand-père. Oui, un la Sesque s'était marié deux fois; sa seconde femme était une Lavignasse. Et comme il avait épousé en premières noces une Péloueyre, par ma belle-mère, nous sommes parents de ce côté-là aussi. . . .[4]

More seriously in *Les Anges noirs* the fact that Andrès and Catherine are first cousins is overlooked when a marriage between them will ensure that the family estates remain undivided; only Gradère shows any concern that it is 'cet amour de la propriété qui implique l'horreur des partages et qui est à l'origine de tant de mariages consanguins'.[5] In many novels inbreeding such as this is shown to lead to physical and mental breakdowns emphasizing the impression that Mauriac creates of a decaying race, and underlining the implication that its values have been misguided.

From the earliest novels there are indications that sons are unlikely to devote themselves wholeheartedly to the family estates. Both Jean-Paul in *L'Enfant chargé de chaînes* and Jacques in *La Robe prétexte* are, as we have seen, closely akin to Mauriac himself; sensitive creatures who discover that their lives move in

---

[1] See, for example, *PL* (*Le Rang*), p. 192.   [2] TD, p. 47.
[3] Op. cit., O.C. t. iv. 459.   [4] Op. cit., O.C. t. i. 440.
[5] Op. cit., p. 47.

new and, for their families, unconventional directions. Daniel
Trassis in *Le Fleuve de feu* prefers to share the shallow pleasures of
Paris with Courrèges even though he is dependent on the income
he receives from his family's estates in the *landes*. But in *Le Baiser
au lépreux*, *Génitrix* and *Destins* the theme of physical decay adds
a further dimension. In each of these novels the older generation
outwits and outmanages its children while in the first and last it
survives them. In *Destins*, for example, Jean Gornac has two sons:
the younger one dies 'demi-fou' while his brother, Prudent,
becomes an alcoholic before being killed in an accident. In turn
his son and living portrait Pierre, quite incapable of imitating his
mother's devotion to the family estates, seeks shelter in religion,
and Jean is left in control. Likewise Jean Péloueyre in *Le Baiser au
lépreux* is the living image of his moribund father: 'Son père le
chérissait comme un souffrant reflet de lui-même, comme son
ombre chétive dans ce monde qu'il traversait en pantoufles ou
étendu au fond d'une alcove parfumée de valérienne et d'éther.'[1]
Yet in spite of his father's poor physical condition it is Jean who
dies prématurely, leaving Jérôme in absolute control after
ensuring that Noémi cannot remarry and thus remove part of the
Péloueyre wealth in the form of a dowry. In *Génitrix* the situation
is strikingly similar. The astute, brutal business attitude that is
second nature to his mother is quite foreign to Fernand, and while
unlike his cousin Jean he remains alive at the close of the novel,
his death is none the less imminent. The depiction of racial
decadence reaches its apotheosis in *Le Sagouin* where both father
and son are physically and mentally unsound, the one arousing the
same revulsion in Paule as the other.[2] This double portrayal of
the same degenerate features, together with Galéas' unhealthy
obsession with the churchyard and his ancestors' tombs, points
warningly to the family's death. Indeed the death shared by father
and son at the end of this novel not only represents the final
stages of the de Cernès family but of all those which populate
Mauriac's novels. Such rottenness at the very heart of a family
results, for the most part as we have seen, from successive con-

[1] Op. cit., O.C. t. i. 151. For the development of the imagery in this novel see
below, Chapter Four.
[2] Op. cit., p. 3.

sanguinous marriages, and it is all the more striking, therefore, that in *Le Baiser au lépreux*, *Génitrix*, and in *Le Sagouin*, the three novels in which the theme is most pronounced, marriage is contracted with an outsider. In the first the union remains sterile, in the second the offspring is prematurely stillborn, and in the third Guillaume is no more than a grotesque miniature of his decadent father. Furthermore in those marriages where physical degeneration of this type is not present—in *Thérèse Desqueyroux* or *Le Mystère Frontenac* for example—the surviving offspring and heir to the family's wealth is invariably a girl ensuring that in name at least the family has ceased to exist.

This theme of gradual decay is conveyed through a symbolic use of the weather and the houses, particularly in the earlier novels, and we shall notice that this is an important feature of Mauriac's writing which in the 1930s forms the essential part of his attempt to bring Grace and Redemption into his work.[1] Winter in *Génitrix* for example accompanies Félicité's death and prepares the way for Fernand's. At the end of the book in particular there is an increasing emphasis on the cold: Fernand 'frémit tout entier et ses dents claquèrent, comme celles de Mathilde mourante'.[2] 'Le froid glaçait les larmes sur ses joues.'[3] Even objects become 'dead': 'Fernand, trébuchant contre des choses mortes.'[4] Similarly in *Le Baiser au lépreux* the coldness and dampness of the church herald Jean's death:

L'humide fraîcheur de la nef la [Noémi] saisit,—ce froid de terre, ce froid de fosse fraîchement ouverte qui étreint les corps vivants dans les églises que le temps enfonce peu à peu et où l'on accède en descendant des marches. Cette toux dont le bruit l'avait éveillée la nuit précédante, de nouveau Noémi l'entendit, mais cette fois répercutée à l'infini par les voûtes.[5]

Diminishing family numbers are also paralleled by a contraction of the house in which they have lived for generations. In *Génitrix* Félicité's bed is brought down to the ground floor and life revolves around the kitchen.[6] In *Destins* after the death of Jean Gornac and

[1] See below, Chapter Four.   [2] Op. cit., O.C. t. i. 400.
[3] Ibid., p. 401.   [4] Ibid., p. 400.
[5] Op. cit., O.C. t. i. 199–200.   [6] G, O.C. t. i. 390–1.

Maria Lagave, Elisabeth rents the Lagave estate, but the house, like its former occupants, is dead: 'Elle visitait souvent cette maison morte, allumait des feux de sarments dans la chambre où Bob avait vécu.'[1]

From such features as these it can be seen that Mauriac's depiction of society is a very particular one; it is a society in the final stages of disintegration, and one which, having created its own material values, has through excessive worship and use of them rendered them sterile. This is not simply an account of the extinction of individuals but of a race as a whole, and Mathilde's words in *Les Anges noirs* could be given a different significance than the one she intends when she remarks: 'Non! La mort n'interrompait rien de ce que les morts avaient commencé.'[2] Perhaps the most appropriate image which Mauriac has ever created to crystallize the emptiness of a situation occurs in *Thérèse Desqueyroux* when Jean Azévédo likens the society around him to a frozen swamp which opens from time to time to engulf yet another unfortunate individual: 'Regardez ... cette immense et uniforme surface de gel où toutes les âmes sont prises; parfois une crevasse découvre l'eau noire: quelqu'un s'est débattu, a disparu; la croûte se referme ... '.[3] Azévédo's bitterness would hardly be out of place in any of Mauriac's novels. From *L'Enfant chargé de chaînes* and *La Robe prétexte* to *Galigaï* and even *L'Agneau*, Mauriac's vision is in appearance one of unqualified pessimism. But it is not sufficient to argue as some have done that the complete absence of spiritual values is a negative admission that they do exist. If he is to agree with Pascal and convince his readers of the danger involved in allowing material well-being to usurp the place which, in his opinion, should belong to spiritual matters he needs as a novelist to be more positive, and it is here that the natural world of his novels becomes so important. In spite of the fact that his personal religious crisis and the attendant discussion of the novel were given open expression in the middle of his career, he was from his earliest works already conscious of the problems involved, but it is not until the 1930s in those novels

---

[1] Op. cit., O.C. t. i. 532.
[2] Op. cit., p. 249.
[3] Op. cit., p. 97.

which in retrospect he has confessed are worthy of the definition *roman catholique* that the natural world (already hinted at in *La Chair et le sang*) becomes the vehicle through which the influence of Grace can be seen to work.

4

THE NATURAL PATTERN OF GRACE

Aucun élément spirituel ne pénétrait le charme de la Pentecôte. Alors que l'enchantement de Noël était né d'une étable, d'un petit enfant sur les genoux de sa mère (ma mère aussi) un enfant que je pouvais tenir dans mes bras, pressé contre ma poitrine. Le mystère de Pâques unissait plus étroitement encore ce que déjà je pressentais de la vie au miracle attendu tout l'hiver de la terre ressuscitée. Cette sourde fermentation, ce sang de Cybèle qui bleuissait les bords du ruisseau, et apparaissait par plaques d'un vert acide à travers la bure des fougères mortes, ce miracle je ne le séparais pas de l'histoire que nous méditions jour après jour, que nous mimions presque grâce à la liturgie de la Semaine Sainte. En revanche, le fait historique de la Pentecôte ne représentait rien pour l'enfant que j'étais. Si quelqu'un m'avait demandé: 'Qu'est-ce que le Saint Esprit?' je n'aurias pas osé répondre: 'une palombe . . .' bien que ce fût au fond ce que je croyais.
FRANÇOIS MAURIAC

BEYOND the widely recognized fact that Mauriac uses the weather as an element to reinforce and to mirror the passions of his characters little attention has been paid to the use he makes of the natural world as a whole. What work that does exist is to be found in the sections on style in the books by Ernst Bendz and Michael Moloney. Each, however, has its limitations. The method adopted by Bendz is statistical. He has made counts of recurring words and phrases, indicating for example that Mauriac uses words such as *boue, souillure,* and *plaie* most frequently in *Le Mal* and *Le Désert de l'amour,* and that with the exception of *Les Anges noirs* they thereafter appear less and less often. He lists areas of vocabulary which have thematic unity— the material world of hygiene and communal life, blood and its association with the crucifixion, fire, and darkness. A similar approach is adopted for Mauriac's images which are neatly divided into six general categories—animal, sea, climate, land, hunting, and religion, especially biblical allusion. Bendz deduces from his mass of evidence that Mauriac's style reflects his early environment, his upbringing, his personal crises, and preoccupations. Moloney adopts a different, more convincing and, in many ways, more worthwhile approach. He contends that Mauriac's images are based on the archetypal elements of water, fire, and earth, and that each can subsume various significances. Water, for example, can in the form of rain act as a barrier; in a storm it is frequently a symbol of generation and sexual desire; as the sea it often symbolizes infinite love. He also points out, as does Bendz, that Mauriac's symbols are not only visual but can also be interpreted through other sense impressions, particularly those of sound and smell. He rightly concludes that Mauriac's writing is most successful when it synthesizes a number of its most prominent stylistic features.

Neither Bendz nor Moloney makes any claim to be writing a comprehensive survey of Mauriac's style. Indeed to do so would require in addition an analysis of a considerable number of different features, yet their work on his images, vocabulary, and symbols which are related to the natural world might usefully be taken a step further in order to show that the manner in which he uses certain devices creates an inner cohesion between subject matter and style, and that this skill is gradually developed until we find two novels, Le Nœud de vipères and Les Anges noirs, constructed in such a way that the metaphysical problems with which they deal are perfectly contained within the cyclic pattern of a natural and animal world.

The two most noticeable stylistic features of any novel by Mauriac are his use of the weather to lend vigour to a human emotion or to provide a context for a particular action, and a repeated motif regularly associated with an individual character or situation. In the early experimental novels these techniques are, as we might expect, only irregularly used. Jacques' return to Ousilanne in La Robe prétexte and his discovery that it is to be sold, coincide with autumn and the dying trees, but this is the only occasion in the novel when this association of season and events is deliberately used by Mauriac for stylistic effect. Occasionally we discover a striking simile or image. Camille is likened to a puppy (p. 40),[1] her hat to a dead bird (p. 22), Marie-Henriette to a

---

[1] In this chapter page references for the texts consulted are included immediately after the quotation.

hen (p. 48 and p. 49), and the basilisk of Saint-Seurin to a 'sombre bête endormie' (p. 56). In *La Chair et le sang*, however, the change of atmosphere from the claustrophobic piety of the previous novel to the open celebration of nature creates a new perspective for Mauriac. Claude and May come together in the heat of the *bordelais* summer which dominates the whole course of the novel.

Il [Claude] ne s'approcha pas, demeura au milieu de la route, immobile, et May le vit tel qu'il était, le pauvre complet veston acheté à Fontenne désormais ne trompa plus ses yeux, elle reconnut le jeune athlète sain, puissant, dévoré de vierge passion et, comme dans les incendies des Landes, le feu d'une cime à l'autre se communique, elle aussi, jeune plante, en face de ce bel arbre embrasé, trembla pour elle et n'osa faire un pas vers lui (p. 198).

And Claude's disturbed emotions after meeting May for the first time are echoed in the abortive storm which sweeps across the country (p. 132). More striking, but less successful since it is so obvious, is the use Mauriac makes of the christo-pagan associations of May's name. Significantly her first communion, the sign of her escape from Protestantism and of her spiritual rebirth, occurs in this very month of May,[1] to be matched within a few days by a bacchic celebration of the grape harvest. Claude too bridges these two worlds; intoxicated 'd'avoir vingt ans et d'être attaché à cette terre bénie' (p. 245) his participation in the Fête-Dieu not only emphasizes their close interrelationship, but also hints (more successfully than in *L'Agneau*) at Claude as a Christ figure:

Le jeudi de la Fête-Dieu, il porta le dais sur la route qui était blanc comme un fleuve de feu. Au long des maisons, les draps plus blancs que la route s'étoilaient de camélias moins blancs que l'hostie rayonnante au centre de toute cette candeur enflammée. Sur les reposoirs, les beaux vases des salons de campagne, les bougeoirs en cuivre des cuisines étaient sortie de la nuit des vieux logis, leurs flammes blêmes, figées, comme rendues immobiles par la présence réelle. Claude, au retour, était heureux que le poids du dais l'accablât. Il voyait, à son approche, des groupes paysans tomber dans la poussière (p. 246).

It is this very involvement of Christian ideas and, in particular in this novel, of conversion, with the pagan notion of fruition that

[1] Chapters 11 and 12.

marks *La Chair et le sang* as the forerunner of Mauriac's Catholic novels in the 1930s. This is not to say that his stylistic devices are already perfected. As the novels written during the following ten years show the process is slow, but increasingly certain in its application.

In his first novels which met with any real degree of public success, *Le Baiser au lépreux* and *Génitrix*, the starkness and brevity of form would hardly seem to allow for any extensive development of these particular aspects of his writing, but in comparison with the earlier novels considerable progress is immediately evident. In *Le Baiser au lépreux* the rain and cold are for the most part the accomplices of the decay and death which are so prominent. Jean Péloueyre's living death is symbolized by the decaying splendour of the *salon* (p. 153) and indeed of the whole house, 'cette maison morte' (p. 197), and he is eventually sealed off from the living world by the winter rain: 'Les pluies de l'hiver finissant enserrèrent la chambre ténébreuse' (p. 208). Through him his young bride Noémi is also affected by the cold and decay; his presence stifles and contaminates her, and it is only away from him that she experiences warmth and an urge to live. This is particularly noticeable of course when the young doctor, who comes to tend first Robert Pieuchon and later Jean himself, is present. His arrival is greeted by 'le soleil de mars' (p. 189) and the disturbance he creates in her emotions is not only likened to a storm—'Elle écoutait comme un orage, s'approcher le gronde-ment d'une voix, des pas dans l'excalier' (p. 195)—but is also accompanied by one: 'le temps est si accablant' (p. 206). Similarly after Jean's death when Noémi sees the doctor again it is 'à la saison la plus dangereuse pour les incendies' (p. 212) but her resistance like the storm or the fires never breaks.

This reflection of human moods and passions in the weather in *Le Baiser au lépreux* occurs only irregularly, however, and in this particular work it is the second of the dominant aspects of Mauriac's writing—the use of a motif—which makes a first and highly successful appearance. Noémi is likened to a flower, a symbol of health and growth, just as Jean is the opposite. Mauriac describes her during the meeting held to discuss her betrothal with Jean: 'Comme dilatée hors du vase une fleur de magnolia, la

F1

robe de Noémi déborde sa chaise. Ce parloir pauvre où Dieu est partout, elle l'imprègne de son odeur de jeune fille, un jour fauve de juillet—pareille à ses trop capiteuses fleurs qu'on ne saurait prudemment laisser dans sa chambre, la nuit' (p. 163). But already Jean's presence is having its effect: 'cette robe un peu fripée qui ne s'épanouirait plus, cette nuque fléchie, fleur moins vivante, fleur déjà coupée' (p. 166). Her growth is halted until Jean leaves for Paris—'il la fuyait pour qu'elle refleurît' (p. 181)—when she experiences for the first time 'l'éclosion en elle d'une femme' (p. 188) which coincides with the warmth of early spring and the first appearance of the young doctor. Her blooming continues until Jean's return; 'sa robe d'organdi s'épanouissait au soleil' (p. 192); she is 'éclatante et fleurissante' (p. 193), but she remains a flower whose seed is never given life. Jean is referred to as an insect, 'cette larve' (p. 164), 'le grillon' (p. 169), as a bat (p. 165), or a night-bird (p. 166) and eventually as a worm which has finally abandoned its corpse (p. 171). He clings to Noémi as an insect clings to a flower, but instead of aiding its reproduction he only succeeds in poisoning its growth.

During the two years separating *Le Baiser au lépreux* from his next novel *Génitrix*, Mauriac's technique shows little development. *Génitrix* rivals *Le Baiser au lépreux* in its harrowing simplicity, the theme of antagonism within a family creating an inward-looking and eventually self-destructive note. Not surprisingly the motif in this novel is war; Félicité and Mathilde frequently refer to one another as *l'ennemie* (e.g. pp. 357, 370, 374, 381, 388) and Félicité is obliged to continue the struggle for the possession of her son even after Mathilde's death: 'Femme positive, ses armes accoutumées ne valaient pas contre un fantôme. Elle ne savait travailler que sur la chair vivante. La tactique de la disparue la déconcertait; tapie en Fernand, elle l'occupait comme une forteresse' (p. 352).

As in *Le Baiser au lépreux* the weather mirrors the action on several occasions. Félicité's passion for her son is as stifling as the heat in the garden:

Cette vieille femme se meurt de ne posséder plus son fils: désir de possession, de domination spirituelle, plus âpre que celui qui emmêle, qui fait se pénétrer, se dévorer deux jeunes corps.

Étouffant, la mère poussa les volets. Le soleil de midi pesait sur le jardin aride. Entre les pelouses poussiéreuses, le sable des allées avait la couleur de la cendre. Le halètement d'un train en partance rappelait une poitrine oppressée. Furibonde, la vieille femme roulant sur ses hanches gagna l'escalier (p. 357).

Later her panic at the thought that Fernand has been completely won over by the memory of his dead wife consumes her like the dry heat threatening the distant pines (p. 363).

While these features remain prominent, it is, as in *Le Baiser au lépreux*, an association of decay and death with the cold that prevails. Fernand an 'enfant pourri' (p. 373) inhabits an isolated 'maison morte' (p. 373) which only shows signs of life when passing trains rattle its decaying joints. As we have already noticed the house also appears to shrink: 'Comme dans un grand corps près de sa fin, la vie se retira des extrémités de la maison et se concentra dans la cuisine' (p. 390). Fernand and his mother take their meals in the kitchen and eventually Félicité's bed is brought down to the ground floor where she dies 'au déclin de l'hiver' (p. 386). Once alone, Fernand follows the same pattern. Like his cousin Jean Péloueyre he is trapped by the rain and mists of the winter days (pp. 396–7), isolated, awaiting death. In this pair of novels the two features of Mauriac's style under discussion remain for the most part separate and appear only irregularly. In the final chapter of *Génitrix*, however, Mauriac achieves something approaching the synthesis which he is to develop over the following years with such success. The house, after the passing of the very last train, is still. The silence is greater than ever before (p. 399), and Fernand is overcome by the cold: 'Il frémit tout entier et ses dents claquèrent . . . ' (p. 400). 'Le froid glaçait les larmes sur ses joues. Son corps frémissait' (p. 401). The house is dead, objects within it are dead, only the plaster statue of the Virgin Mary, heralding the return of the servant Marie de Lados and symbolizing Fernand's resignation to God's will, offers any comfort.

The impression made by these two short works depends very largely on the slightness of their size in comparison with the sharpness and even, at times, brutality of their content. In spite of the first four novels they are in many ways embryo works,

containing in germ the stylistic skills which Mauriac has yet to
perfect and work into a more intricate pattern. The first signs
of this appear in *Le Désert de l'amour* and *Thérèse Desqueyroux* each
of which shows a considerable advance in technique. Throughout
Le Désert de l'amour we are made aware of the struggle for
existence, and for the first time Mauriac explores human relationships in terms of a natural and animal world. Already in *Génitrix*
Félicité's desire to possess her son was instinctive. In *Le Désert de
l'amour* such behaviour is explored once more and points as it will in
Les Anges noirs, to the type of role born frequently of frustration and
generally held by women in Mauriac's novels. Madeleine Basque
experiences a sexual hunger for her husband; it is, says Mauriac,
as if 'elle eût appartenu à une espèce différente des autres animaux,
où le mâle et non le femelle eût été odorant pour attirer la complice
à travers l'ombre' (p. 21). She defies her father for the sake of 'le
mâle qui l'appelait' (p. 58), her existence with whom is based
wholly on instincts: 'Le lit immense s'ouvrait dans l'ombre devant
le couple. Ils y allaient comme ils se mettaient à table à midi et à
huit heures: le moment d'avoir faim' (p. 60). The principal interest
of *Le Désert de l'amour*, however, lies in Raymond's brief en-
counter with Maria Cross, and in the marked effect that this has on
the rest of his life. This, however, is not due as Raymond thinks
to the hurt that his pride has suffered, but to the fact that he was
rejected by her on the threshold of manhood. He belongs to 'ce
troupeau d'enfants près de mourir, et d'hommes près de naître.
Sous la poussée d'une germination douloureuse, la jeune forêt
humaine s'étirait en quelques mois, grêle et souffrante' (p. 38),
and on a number of occasions Mauriac emphasizes the stirrings of
this new growth within Raymond—the unexpected nose bleeds
(p. 60) or the change in his appearance which goes unnoticed by
his family (p. 71). He is described variously as a young animal
(p. 113), a wild bird (p. 136 and p. 137), a young dog (p. 167) and,
perhaps more significantly, as a goat (p. 150). Noticeable too is
the fact that this crucial period of Raymond Courrège's life
occurs during the spring. He first meets Maria Cross 'à la fin de
janvier, alors qu'en ces régions déjà l'hiver décline' (p. 61). It is a
season of mists and suspense before the rite of spring begins:
'déjà la brume recelait cette douceur secrète de la saison qui

approchait. La terre était nue mais elle ne dormait pas' (p. 64). The period of incubation is nearing its end with the warmth of approaching spring and the presence of Maria Cross. Mauriac blends the images together—the natural and the human—'la brume amassée dans cette âme peu à peu se dissipait sous cette attention grave, toujours muette . . . ' (p. 72). As the fatal meeting between Maria and Raymond draws near, so Mauriac replaces the quiet mists of dying winter and the gradual stirrings of spring by the threatening skies of summer: 'Tous ces jours-là, les vents de l'Ouest et du Sud traînèrent après eux des masses obscures, des légions grondantes qui, près de fondre, soudain hésitaient, tournaient autour des cimes fascinées, puis disparaissaient, laissant derrière elles cette fraîcheur de quand il a plu quelque part' (pp. 164–5). Raymond's visit to Maria is accompanied by such weather: 'il fait étouffant. D'ailleurs j'entends l'orage . . . ' (p. 172), but like his desire it never materializes. In this novel Mauriac comes close to achieving on a large scale the type of synthesis which appeared briefly in the final chapter of *Génitrix*, and having done so it is all the more noticeable that in his next novel, *Thérèse Desqueyroux*, he should use a motif which is quite independent of any cyclic natural pattern and which is so dominant in fact that it causes the latter rather to be overlooked. On occasions of course, the now familiar pattern can still be traced. Thérèse's hostility towards her husband and her attempt to poison him are nourished by the fierce heat of the *bordelais* summer: 'Déjà régnait, en ce matin de juillet, une chaleur sulfureuse' (p. 51), 'Les premières chaleurs accablaient Thérèse. . . . Des semaines se succédèrent sans que tombât une goutte d'eau' (p. 115). Autumn and winter witness her imprisonment at Argelouse: 'une pluie menue, serrée, ruisselait sur les tuiles des communs, sur les feuilles encore épaisses de chênes' (p. 151); 'En ces jours les plus courts de l'année, la pluie épaisse unifie le temps, confond les heures; un crépuscule rejoint l'autre dans le silence immuable' (p. 157). Eventually spring greets the freedom to live in Paris that Bernard grants her. But in *Thérèse Desqueyroux* this pattern remains for the most part unobtrusive, hidden behind the mass of references to Thérèse's environment as a prison and to her struggle to escape: 'Au plus épais d'une famille, elle allait couver, pareille à un feu sournois qui rampe sous la brande, embrase un pin, puis l'autre, puis de proche en proche crée une forêt de torches' (p. 45). Unlike the fire, however, Thérèse's attempts are doomed to failure, the family into which she has married proves too strong. This is the motif that dominates the whole novel, appearing sometimes in the presence of the encircling pines (pp. 100, 130, 136), in the rain (p. 109), or in Azévédo's previously quoted image of the frozen swamp. Eventually her prison is opened: 'il lui semblait que les pins s'écartaient, ouvraient leurs rangs, lui faisaient signe de prendre le large' (p. 175). But her escape is only temporary; she is liberated from one prison only to be cast into another, Parisian society, 'un fleuve de boue et de corps pressés' (p. 181).

Such techniques, by now recognizable features of any novel by Mauriac, continue beyond the critical period marked by *Souffrances et bonheur du chrétien* to provide the vehicle for the introduction of Grace, and also an answer to those like Gide who accused Mauriac of attempting to serve both God and Mammon. Many critics following in the wake of Charles du Bos see Mauriac's first real achievement in *Le Nœud de vipères*. Certainly in this work he probes into the innermost recesses of a human mind and follows the struggle that exists within Louis himself and between him and those closest to him. Given this situation it is not surprising to rediscover the motif of war that had appeared in *Génitrix* now conveyed in a series of images which stretches from the title itself to the simple vocabulary of war—*tenir sur ses gardes, guerre ouverte, battre en retraite*. But *Le Nœud de vipères* is remarkable above all for the manner in which, for the first time, Mauriac incorporates the majority of his images within the dominant motifs of enmity and freedom, and in so doing gives the book an inner tension which in earlier works had at best only been suggested. There are, of course, exceptions to this rule, but they are few and appear only to colour or to sharpen a particular observation. Louis glimpses some nearby roofs and compares them to vividly coloured flowers or feathers; his writing slants like pine trees before the wind; Isa at one point is described as 'une vieille machine' (p. 152) and Louis' hatred as a tired horse. Occasionally an extended image, such as that involving the notion of spiritual recovery and the grape harvest, on p. 127, or of sailing, on p. 66, may be found, but in general these are few.

As Vincent Tartella has indicated in an interesting study of the imagery of this novel, Louis refers to the title phrase on four occasions.[1] All are entangled by plots and counterplots, and, until Louis can cut through the knot, release is impossible. Tartella also draws our attention to the 'more subtle manifestations'[2] of the image—the 'boa' worn by Marinette and the money belt which Louis offers Luc for example. But there are other, extended uses which he ignores, particularly the reference to circles and, by extension, to the oppressiveness of the room in which Louis finds himself, surrounded by the freedom of the natural world outside. Through his descriptions of the family Louis gives the impression of being both confined and judged:

'la famille assise en rond' (p. 67); 'cette meute familiale assise en rond' (p. 74); 'le cercle de famille se resserre autour de mon lit' (p. 116); 'le nœud de vipères est en dehors de moi; elles sont sorties de moi et elles s'enroulaient, cette nuit, elles formaient ce cercle hideux au bas du perron' (pp. 158–9).

His room, to which he is confined at Calèse, the hotel rooms when he first meets Isa's family, later, the rue Bréa in Paris, and even the church of St. Germain des Prés, associated as it is with Hubert's plots, underline this theme of the oppression which Louis has to suffer, though at the end his imprisonment becomes a refuge.

In contrast we find that the notion of regeneration is carried by the frequent references to water and to the freedom of young animals. Again Tartella has a number of pertinent observations on the use which Mauraic makes of water.[3] He draws our attention to the thawing (*détente; sources délivrées* (p. 35)) of Louis' nature when he first meets Isa; his spiritual aridity and the drying up of his emotions after the Rodolphe incident; to Louis' description of the hate in his heart moving to and fro like a tide; to his *millions liquides* (p. 74). At the same time water also symbolizes purity, the reference to a spring appearing in the description of both Luc and Marie, while at the close of his journal Louis too is

[1] Vincent Tartella, 'Thematic imagery in Mauriac's *Vipers' Tangle*', *Renascence*, XVII, 4, p. 196.
[2] Ibid., p. 196.   [3] Ibid., pp. 197–9.

surrounded by the 'éternelle pluie'; the cleansing process of his regeneration has begun.

As rain water forms part of the overall seasonal pattern which plays such an important role towards the end of Louis' life, so it is here too in particular that the more detailed references to the natural and animal world come to form an integral part of a wider motif. Like so many characters in earlier novels the family here is defined in animal terms, 'la meute familiale'; Phili who has stalked Janine as a beast of prey with one eye always to her dowry is a 'jeune loup'; Janine herself who submits to her tasks with the numbed willingness of a faithful dog has 'des yeux de bête fidèle' (p. 225); Hubert as a victim is a 'pauvre larve' ready to be crushed or a mouse, and, when pathetically grateful to Louis for his allowance, a dog. In each case Mauriac is careful in his choice, and we find that his descriptions of Luc and Marie are similarly phrased, their freshness and innocence like Noémi's in *Le Baiser au lépreux* mirrored in the references to them both as birds (pp. 80, 121) and also to Luc as a fawn (p. 121). They are the victims of society, hunted creatures whose purity and innocence are only preserved through an early death.

It is arguable that by creating such analogies between his characters and certain animals in this way Mauriac is guilty of an over simplification. We are constantly reminded of what each is intended to represent and hence of the part he or she is to play in the book as a whole: some hunt, others are hunted. But while such criticism may be valid for some of his earlier writing, to level it against *Le Nœud de vipères* would be to attack the system of the book as a whole. Mauriac has created a complex system of images and motifs which not only carries the book along at its most superficial level of interpretation, but which acts as a vehicle for its spiritual intention.

Behind the family intrigues the weather plays out its accompaniment; heat as in *Thérèse Desqueyroux* heralds disruption. The memory of Rodolphe, the starting point of the disharmony in Louis and Isa's marriage, is introduced at the same time as a threat of fire: 'Le vent du sud qui traverse les Landes, portait jusqu'à notre lit l'odeur d'un incendie' (pp. 16, 17). Further, the attraction which Marinette and Louis feel secretly for one another burns within them unconfessed: 'Ainsi demeurions-nous l'un près de l'autre, au bord de cette cuve immense où la vendange future fermentait dans le soleil des feuilles bleuies' (pp. 102, 103). But it is Louis' own spiritual progression which is echoed most consistently in the weather. Stripped finally of his wealth and, in his own mind at least, at peace with his family he is on the point of spiritual rebirth (p. 207). The autumn rains begin their symbolic cleansing, and Louis feels himself 'pénétré jusqu'au cœur par la paix qui remplissait la terre' (p. 214). His death, which finally occurs in November as the cold closes in on him just as it did on Fernand in *Génitrix*, is shared by the vines with which he has been associated and identified throughout the novel, but like theirs his death is only temporary; Louis' salvation is as certain as the next stage in the cyclic pattern of nature of which he has become a part. In this way Mauriac draws the two worlds together. Louis' spiritual rebirth is as much an extension of the natural pattern of the book as it is of any involved confession or misunderstanding if not more so. His success is made clear when the following novel *Le Mystère Frontenac* only continues the pattern in the most superficial manner. The motif of the 'sacred family'[1] is easily enough observable, but nowhere is it as dominant or as impressive as the 'prison' motif, in *Thérèse Desqueyroux* for example. Similarly, though autumn heralds the disintegration of the family at the close of both parts of the novel, the problems of conversion or of the intervention of Grace do not arise, and no significant overall pattern emerges as in *Le Nœud de vipères* or more notice-ably three years later in *Les Anges noirs*.[2]

    While undoubtedly displaying considerable weaknesses this novel has been sorely neglected, for it offers the type of synthesis that Mauriac, with varying success, had been striving after for a number of years. Here, but with more force than in *Le Nœud de vipères*, the seasonal and natural cycle incorporates the dominant motif, to produce a pattern of existence which carries through the notion of Gradère's redemption. This motif, once again the instinctive, basically animal nature of human beings, is traced

---

[1] See below, Chapter Five.
[2] For a fuller discussion of this novel see my study, *'Les Anges noirs' de François Mauriac. Une étude critique*, Paris, 1969.

through Mauriac's descriptions of his characters' physical appearance and in their relationships with one another. Our attention is drawn to Adila's body (p. 13); Catherine's gaze is 'très vif et pourtant animal' (p. 76), Andrès has 'une nature simple, animale' (p. 190), Forcas 'une figure de jeune brute' (p. 237) with its 'front de petit buffle' (p. 80), while Desbats 'court comme un rat dans la maison' (p. 68). In the same way in which words like *accabler*, *étouffer*, and *couver* reinforce the general oppressive hot-house atmosphere in *Thérèse Desqueyroux* so too in *Les Anges noirs* we find *roder*, *tapi*, *au gîte*, and *flairer*. In addition all the members of the family in the château, like the society of Liogeats as a whole, obey the 'mobiles simples de l'animalité'. Catherine is attracted to Andrès by 'cet appétit qu'elle avait de lui et qu'elle savait mal dissimuler' (p. 243); Mathilde gives Gradère her support because she secretly hopes that she will one day marry Andrès; Tota only finds him attractive in the half light: 'il ne lui plaisait que dans les ténèbres, lorsqu'il devenait une créature sans visage, défendue contre toute expression stupide ou basse,—un corps décapité dans l'ombre' (p. 117).

Such instinctive behaviour as this, already present in *Le Désert de l'amour* and *Le Nœud de vipères*, fits more easily into this novel where the natural and seasonal pattern of life is more clearly emphasized. The action as distinct from any reported events in Gradère's *Journal* is concerned with intrigue and murder, and not surprisingly is worked out during the dark months of winter, hidden from the rest of the world by a curtain of incessant rain: 'Pendant des semaines peut-être cette pluie enserrait la maison, le parc, les séparait des autres hommes' (p. 135). Rain accompanies the action almost continuously, becoming more and more intense through the scenes of Aline's arrival and her murder. However, it ceases to be an accomplice to the crime once committed, and instead assumes the power to cleanse. With this change the unnatural darkness of Liogeats also disappears. Night, already referred to as 'pure et froide' (p. 129) in comparison with the dark intrigues inside the house, is now given greater prominence. Moonlight, which appears briefly upon Gradère's arrival symbolizing the purity of Liogeats not yet corrupted by his presence, reappears towards the close of the novel. It lights his path to the presbytery (p. 232) and is also a symbol of divine blessing (p. 250). Indeed all is purified. The rain has ceased, the sky is washed clear; the mists which had innocently witnessed Gradère's arrival are now pure again, the only remaining evil being that trapped within Desbats' room to which Mathilde is bound by her penance: 'elle étouffait dans cette chambre fétide. L'odeur de fumée et d'urine l'asphyxiait. Une vitre la séparait de ce rafraîchissement, de ce fleuve lacté, de cette nuit ruisselante sur les derniers lilas, sur les premières aubépines' (p. 246). All in fact, as Andrès discovers, is blessed once more with 'cette fraîcheur édénique d'après le chaos' (p. 245). After the dark weeks of winter, life begins anew, spring follows winter, spiritual rebirth follows death. After more than fifty years in the shadow of the Devil, Gradère finds salvation.

With *Le Nœud de vipères* and *Les Anges noirs* Mauriac comes near to achieving what ten years earlier both he and Bernanos had considered an impossibility—the novel about Grace. Grace does not appear in any supernatural form to regulate events, but it is seen to shape the destinies of Louis and Gradère. Mauriac has placed a spiritual matter in what is an essentially pagan context and in so doing has not so much avoided the more usual techniques associated with Catholic literature as added to them. His traditional themes and material remain, even at times appearing more sombre and despairing than before, but his intention has found a constant means of expression. It is as though the underlying pattern of these novels becomes a massive symbol which must be grasped before the meaning of the book can emerge. In this way Mauriac is able to face Gide and the hostile critic who is now powerless to separate the faith from the writing and attack one at the expense of the other. The last minute appearance of the plaster statue in *Génitrix* or Gisèle de Plailly's conversion in *Le Fleuve de feu* lack the power to carry the rest of the novel; they are jerked in to recast a frame of reference which has been becoming less and less Catholic. Certainly the critic can object to the letters which close *Le Nœud de vipères* or the play on Gradère's supernatural qualities in *Les Anges noirs*, but he cannot deny that these novels have a new inner cohesion, an inner tension which does not simply illustrate the workings of Grace, but, in order to be complete, actually requires it. Unfortunately Mauriac's peak of achievement was short lived. In spite of a number of arresting episodes, *La Fin de la nuit* attacked by Sartre, *La Pharisienne* Mauriac's reply, and *Les Chemins de la mer* lack this total quality of their immediate predecessors. The cyclic and seasonal pattern perfected over the years becomes increasingly less striking until it is completely absent from his last novel, *L'Agneau*, which turns in a new and unsuccessful direction.

It may be argued, therefore, that Mauriac's achievement was short lived and indeed that it came at the point in his career when his interests began to move in new directions, towards journalism and the theatre. At the same time *L'Agneau*, published nearly twenty years after *Le Nœud de vipères* and *Les Anges noirs*, does not represent an isolated attempt to resolve the problem of the Catholic novel in one particular way. Already in *Le Mystère Frontenac* Mauriac had set out to redress his picture of humanity by under-lining the value of human love as a reflection of divine love, and together these two novels deserve our attention in order to see how the traditional features of his writing proved too strong to be easily altered, and how his own view that didactic literature was inevitably doomed proved correct.

5

MAURIAC'S ENCHANTED FAMILY

IF we are to judge from the principal critical attitudes to *Le Mystère Frontenac* Mauriac's intentions would appear to be wholly justified. This, it was argued, was no ordinary *roman mauriacien* for much of the bitterness of his earlier vision of humanity seemed to have gone and after *Le Nœud de vipères* in particular it appeared to be a quiet, fairly harmless work unlikely to irritate many critics and certainly not the more demanding Catholic ones. Immediate reaction expressed through reviews in newspapers and periodicals was, typically enough, conservative and unexciting, recounting the plot, indicating Mauriac's presentation of a family *mystique*, making general observations about his work and even the odd error. Yet some critics seem to have been nearer a more useful evaluation than they perhaps imagined; André Rousseaux in *Le Figaro* for example, who noticed the strong theme of decadence and in his review compared *Le Mystère Frontenac* with Thomas Mann's *Buddenbrooks*: 'L'un et l'autre nous représentent la décadence d'une famille,'[1] or Louis de Mondadon in *Etudes* who drew attention to the significance of the family for a Catholic audience. A third critic, Edmond Jaloux, who reviewed the novel for *Les Nouvelles littéraires* and in the same year wrote about it in his preface to Mauriac's *Le Romancier et ses personnages*, sounded the note that was to characterize most of the subsequent discussions. It was, he said, 'Un repos, une oasis [...] moins un roman qu'une confession romancée qui se trouve [...] un peu à l'écart de la grande voie.'[2] Since then, critics have continued to consider *Le Mystére Frontenac* as an exception. Alain Palante refers to it as 'l'exceptionnel et unique *Mystére Frontenac*';[3] Emile Rideau as 'Une parenthèse, une trêve dans l'œuvre de Mauriac',[4] while Jacques Robichon defines it as

[1] Op. cit., 22 February 1933, p. 5. [2] Op. cit., Paris, 1933, p. 10.
[3] *Mauriac, le roman et la vie*, p. 176. [4] *Comment lire François Mauriac*, p. 68.

'l'ouvrage le plus spontané de toute l'architecture mauriacienne, celui [. . .] qui a le plus certainement échappé à la grande usine du roman mauriacien'.[1] Others who have written about Mauriac's work see the novel as a poetic antidote to earlier themes, while Conor Cruise O'Brien regards it more severely as 'a terrible setback'.[2] No critics, however, have examined this novel in the detail that it demands in order to discover what evidence there is for considering it in this manner, nor on the other hand have they estimated to what extent it can be aligned with other novels of the 1930s. All of them seem to sense that it is in some way different, but in their eagerness to prove their point they have neglected the equally important traditional features of Mauriac's writing.

In the *Préface* to the fourth volume of his *Œuvres complètes*, Mauriac admits that he was inspired to write *Le Mystère Frontenac* by the love and affection shown to him by his family and relations at the time a throat infection was, for a moment, thought to be cancer. Had he died, he says, he would not have wished posterity to have had *Le Nœud de vipères* as his last word:

J'ai conçu *Le Mystère Frontenac* comme un hymne à la famille au lendemain d'une grave opération et de la maladie durant laquelle les miens m'avaient entouré d'une sollicitude si tendre. Si j'avais dû mourir, je n'aurais pas voulu que *Le Nœud de vipères* fût le dernier de mes livres.

And he goes on, 'Avec *Le Mystère Frontenac* je faisais amende honorable à la race.'[3] But did he? In spite of his efforts is Mauriac's portrait of a bourgeois family in this novel—albeit a transposition of his own—essentially different from his traditional one, and, more importantly, does he really succeed in convincing us?

By 1933 Mauriac had already completed at least a dozen pieces of imaginative writing in which the faults and weaknesses of the bourgeois family were, as we have seen, cruelly exposed. Obsession with material wealth at the expense of spiritual values, the creation of a faceless society which swallows any individual who should attempt to assert himself, the whole range of the 'mystiques sans dieu' that stand out in *Le Désert de l'amour* are accepted features. Individual families too are cells of intrigue,

---

[1] *François Mauriac*, p. 95.   [2] *Maria Cross*, p. 11.   [3] Op. cit., p. 11.

corruption and disruption, fathers cynically plan their offspring, nephews seek to break into their cousins' inheritance, and wives and mothers strive desperately and in vain to retain some sort of affectionate bond with the children they have been required to produce. Families are dying and offspring are for the most part mad, moribund, or at best female. In face of this Mauriac needed a strong stimulant indeed to make his recantation convincing, and as we shall see the fact that he felt guilty about his earlier bitterness was not really enough.

The problem with *Le Mystère Frontenac* as with all the novels written during the thirties is that which emerged from *Le Romancier et ses personnages*: the need to involve religion in such a way that while the intended interpretation of the work is indicated clearly enough, any criticism of didacticism or of Mauriac's adoption of an arbitrary standpoint is avoided. In *Le Nœud de vipères* and *Les Anges noirs* the gradual discovery of faith and the theme of redemption are the crucial matters; in this novel Mauriac sets out to impose a family *mystique* which not only emphasizes the need to subordinate mortal to divine love—the problem so thoroughly explored a few years earlier in *Souffrances et bonheur du chrétien*—but also attempts to endow the family with a certain quasi religious significance of its own. Any examination of *Le Mystère Frontenac* must therefore be carried out on two levels: the first to examine the extent to which Mauriac's apology for the family is conditioned by the nature of his customary attitude, and secondly to see how and with what success he has implanted the religious element.

As in earlier novels the family group in *Le Mystère Frontenac* can be divided into those who are related by blood and those who have already entered or attempt to enter it from the outside through marriage. Hence we find that Michel and Xavier's relationship is echoed in that of Yves and Jean-Louis,[1] while Xavier as a true Frontenac has, on occasions, a greater sense of belonging to the family than Blanche who has only found her way in by her marriage to Michel. The kind of difficulty which she experiences appears in a more acute form in the relationships of Joséfa and Madeleine with Xavier and Jean-Louis. Xavier's

[1] See, for example, p. 52.

sense of family duty becomes clear in his reaction to Blanche's practical suggestion that the half-witted tante Félicia should be removed to a home. Nothing could be more inconceivable:

Moi vivant—cria-t-il d'une voix aigüe—tante Félicia ne quittera pas la maison de famille. Jamais la volonté de mon père ne sera violée. Il ne s'est jamais séparé de sa sœur . . . [1]

His respect for Félicia is absolute:

Il la baisait au front avec un tendre respect, car ce monstre s'appelait Félicia Frontenac. C'était une Frontenac, la propre sœur de son père, la survivante.[2]

This mixture of respect and duty is extended into his relationships with his nephews, in whom he finds physical and spiritual traces of his dead brother. Since Michel's death he has generously agreed to manage his sister-in-law's estates for her, ensuring that her family would always be well provided for. But between them there is always a barrier. Xavier can never regard Blanche in any way other than as Michel's wife and mother of his children; her role is purely functional:

Elle n'existait à ses yeux qu'en fonction des petits Frontenac. Il ne pensait jamais à sa belle-soeur comme à une jeune femme solitaire, capable d'éprouver de la tristesse, du désespoir. Sa destinée ne l'intéressait en rien. Pourvu qu'elle ne se remariât pas et qu'elle élevât les enfants de Michel, il ne se posait guère de question à son sujet.[3]

With his nephews and nieces, however, his relationship is quite different, and when Blanche is called away to care for her sick mother, Xavier and the children enjoy an idyllic sharing of adolescence. On her return Blanche immediately notices a change: 'il régnait entre les neveux et l'oncle, une complicité, des plaisanteries occultes, des mots à double entente, tout un mystère où elle n'entrait pas'.[4]

Even so Xavier's sense of devotion and loyalty to the family may be said to have its limits; though ashamed of it,[5] he does not feel himself in any way prevented from conducting an affair with an ordinary and not very attractive 'petite dame' as Joséfa is rather

[1] Ibid., p. 23.   [2] Ibid., p. 18.   [3] Ibid., p. 11 and p. 12.
[4] Ibid., p. 95.   [5] Ibid., p. 42.

disparagingly called by Alfred. Mistress she must remain, however, and Blanche's tactful suggestion that Xavier might marry is as quickly rejected as were her plans for Félicia. It is not simply a question of social unsuitability; more important is that marriage to Joséfa would create a breach in the Frontenac strength. Xavier's world, like Jérôme Péloueyre's or Pierre Gornac's, is a male world in which women with few exceptions are either ground into submission or choose to sink their personality in the tasks demanded of them. Predictably enough Maria and Danièle, the two Frontenac daughters, have only shadowy roles, leaving their clan by marriage, only reappearing infrequently and with no significant effect. The three boys on the other hand, Jean-Louis, José and Yves, all, in varying degrees, feel the need and the desire to participate in their family mystique. José, in spite of his temporary aberrations, is more ready than any to devote himself unquestioningly to his family's wealth and property, for him, as for the majority of Mauriac's characters, the source of all happiness: 'José n'avait d'autre ambition que de devenir "le paysan de la famille".'[1] He is never more at home than when roaming through the pine forests with his dog or when setting traps for eels. Such devotion would have gone a long way to compensate for any lack of intelligence, and it is ironic and significant that he should be killed in battle before he has the chance to prove his worth. Jean-Louis and Yves, however, are quite different. Each of them can entertain quite clearly the idea of another form of existence and are therefore contravening their uncle's and their mother's wishes. As we shall see, only Yves manages to escape from the material pressure to conform and it is through him that Mauriac attempts to introduce his idea of an ideal family love. For the moment the case of Jean-Louis is more relevant. His adolescent ambition to achieve both the *agrégation* and a *doctorat* in philosophy die slowly. At first he maintains to his mother that the family business has no attraction for him at all: 'j'ai nullement l'intention d'entrer dans les affaires. . . . Le commerce ne m' intéresse pas.'[2] But his confidence gradually crumbles before his elders' persuasive tactics and his philosophic intentions find only an abortive expression in an attempt to promote some form of social catholic

[1] Ibid., p. 50.   [2] Ibid., p. 98.

programme for his workers. His conditioning is complete when he realizes that necessity and duty must take precedence over any individual or personal happiness:

Il ne s'agit pas de bonheur, pour eux—dit Jean-Louis—mais d'agir en vue du bien commun et dans l'intérêt de la famille. Non, il ne s'agit pas de bonheur. . . . Le bonheur. . . . J'ai toujours vu à maman cette figure pleine de tourment et d'angoisse. . . . Si papa avait vécu, je pense que c'eût été pareil. . . . Non, pas le bonheur; mais le devoir . . . une certaine forme du devoir, devant laquelle ils n'hésitent jamais. . . . Et le terrible, mon petit, c'est que je les comprends.[1]

As far as Jean-Louis is concerned the family maxim has not been without avail: 'Tu feras ce qu'ont fait ton père et ton grand-père'.[2]

The influence of Mauriac's own home on the description of the Frontenac family is more evident when we move beyond this blood relationship to the wider notion of the family group including the wife brought in by marriage. Here, however, there is some ambiguity, for Xavier, the last of the 'vieux Frontenac', Blanche can never really belong to the family in the way that Michel or the unmarried Félicia have done; she must remain 'une demoiselle Arnaud-Miqueu, une personne accomplie, mais venue du dehors'.[3] To a certain extent she occupies in this novel the place that Mathilde had in Génitrix or Louis in Le Nœud de vipères. But Xavier does not represent the present generation. Jean-Louis' academic interests and Yves' literary ambitions already show that their elders' attitudes and convictions are not to remain unchallenged, and even though she is their mother it is not surprising that some change should occur in the traditional family attitudes to outsiders. In spite of the peculiar bond created between the children and their uncle during her absence, Blanche is accepted much more readily by the younger generation as a true Frontenac than by her elders or contemporaries, and Mauriac is at pains to show that family love finds a special expression in the relationship between Blanche and her children. Does not Yves state that Dussol's picture of her as an astute business woman is only an unreal caricature: 'il ne pouvait conjurer cette

[1] Ibid., p. 104.   [2] Ibid., p. 98.   [3] Ibid., p. 22.

caricature, que Dussol lui imposait, de sa mère telle qu'elle apparaissait aux autres, dépouillée du mystère Frontenac.'?[1] It is of course essential to Mauriac that Blanche should appear central to the *mystère* since at the close of the book he presents us with a vision of the eternally united mother and children. None the less it is difficult to reconcile the Blanche who in spite of everything holds the traditional Mauriac position of an outsider with Blanche the initiate. Mauriac suggests that he is aware of this by introducing yet another autobiographical detail, and also by asking us to consider the five Frontenac children for the most part through Blanche's eyes.

As we saw in Chapter Two, marriage in the bourgeois society of Mauriac's novels is very rarely founded on affection, but Blanche and Michel seem to have been an exception. Mauriac is of course on dangerous ground, since he could hardly have written his hymn to a family so evidently based on his own and yet have given too sombre a picture of the parents. Mauriac's father died, we recall, when François was only twenty months old, and since Michel has suffered the same fate we have no evidence whatsoever with which to challenge the apparent harmony of his marriage with Blanche.[2] More important, however, is the way in which Mauriac details Blanche's devotion to her children. Her anxiety over Xavier's care for the half-witted Félicia is not only a monetary one. She is also concerned that the children's prospects of marriage should not be compromised by a rumour of hereditary family insanity.[3] She is quick to defend her brother-in-law when her own family are gently scornful of his affair with Joséfa.[4] Above all she is concerned with the material well-being of her children; Dussol praises her astute business sense,[5] she finds herself wondering who would inherit her mother's house if she dies,[6] she is very aware of the potential value of Madeleine's dowry and,[7] obsessed by the idea that she may have cancer, she lumps material and spiritual values together: 'elle pensait à

[1] Ibid., p. 190.
[2] Ibid., p. 122. Blanche continues to wear a brooch, 'un B et un F entrelacés'.
[3] Ibid., p. 26.
[4] Ibid., pp. 34–5. 'L'esprit Frontenac l'avait envahie tout entière'.
[5] Ibid., p. 187.   [6] Ibid., p. 80.
[7] Ibid., p. 55.

l'agonie, à la mort, au jugement de Dieu, au partage des propriétés'.[1]

Yet so indelible are the traditional features of the bourgeois family in Mauriac's imaginative writing that he is obliged ultimately to endow the Frontenac family with a supernatural unity in an attempt to prevent Blanche being automatically considered as the outsider. Her sense of devotion and her self-sacrifice are not enough, and the inevitable limitations to the type of relationship which she enjoys with her family are picked out more clearly in the roles of Joséfa and Madeleine, both of whom attempt, in the latter case with success, to enter the Frontenac clan by marriage.

From the outset Joséfa is less likely to succeed than Madeleine Cazavieilh who at least has wealth and social status on her side. Xavier's shame at his inability to do without her and his pleasure when their proposed trip to Switzerland has to be cancelled is only to be expected, though his final rejection of her is more difficult to accept, and must be attributed, at least in part, to his illness and the presence of his nephews and nieces.[2] On the other hand it is equally hard to understand Jean-Louis' willingness to admit Joséfa to the *mystère*, unless we view this as yet another piece of evidence for the gradual erosion of the family's hitherto rigid social requirements and distinctions. Madeleine has none of Joséfa's disadvantages; she is wealthy and already distantly related to the Frontenac children, the perfect prerequisites for any match in this society, ensuring that materially at least neither Jean-Louis nor his family will lose anything by his marrying her. Even in this novel, however, the idea of convenience is never far away, and it is always implied that Jean-Louis and Madeleine live together because it is expected of them, rather than because they have chosen to do so out of mutual affection. Madeleine remains blissfully indifferent to her husband's problems, adopting an air of quiet resignation:

Madeleine sourit d'un air malin et entendu, haussa les épaules et se resservit. Elle n'était pas une Frontenac; à quoi bon insister? Elle ne comprendrait pas. Elle n'était pas une Frontenac.[3]

[1] Ibid., p. 117.   [2] Ibid., p. 225.   [3] Ibid., p. 151.

In a way that is typical of the majority of mothers in Mauriac's novels she has settled into a life of caring for her child instead of her husband. Like Anne de la Trave her sole interest and duty in life has been to marry. She has no vision beyond her role as a childbearer and is totally indifferent to Jean-Louis' ambitions:

Et elle, indifférente aux noms qu'il citait, n'osait lui poser la seule question qui l'intéressât: attendrait-il, pour se marier, d'avoir fini ce travail? La préparation d'une thèse était-elle compatible avec l'état de mariage?[1]

Her equanimity during their engagement—'elle était paisible, elle attendait'[2]—already fixes the emptiness, the 'pauvre bonheur' as Yves calls it, of their married life together. 'Il chérissait profondément Madeleine'[3] is not the same as 'Il aimait profondément Madeleine', and it is hardly surprising that virtuous as he is, Jean-Louis should be tempted by other women.

If at this juncture we ignore the nature of the *mystère* itself, it is useful to consider what emerges from this network of human relations and attempt to evaluate it in terms of similar material in other novels. The Frontenac family is typical of the *bordelais* society which we examined earlier; its existence is largely conditioned by its wealth, children are married carefully, ambitions, except in the case of Yves, are quickly stifled. Religion is never prominent, but the children have been brought up in a Christian household and at least we feel that spiritual values are genuine even if Blanche should align them with material ones. Seen in these terms the Frontenac family in essence is not very different from the Péloueyre, the Gornac, or the Desqueyroux. We also find that other traditional features of Mauriac's imaginative writing make their appearance throughout the novel. Félicia like Fernand Cazenave or Jean Péloueyre inhabits a 'grande maison morte', the pines which witnessed the adolescence of the Frontenac children are at the close of the novel either dying or have been cut down; so too have the alders.[4] Already in the first part of the book the family group is seen to be breaking up,[5] and in Part Two

---

[1] Ibid., p. 58.   [2] Ibid., p. 115.   [3] Ibid., p. 249.
[4] Ibid., p. 247 and p. 197.
[5] Ibid., p. 125, 'déjà la vie dispersait le groupe serré des garçons'.

dispersion becomes finalized in death. Xavier and Blanche both die, Yves' and José's days are numbered and Jean-Louis' future unfaithfulness is already recorded. The end of the Frontenac family is in sight. Jean-Louis is trapped by the family business 'comme dans une fosse où il eût été pris à jamais';[1] Xavier considers his nephews and nieces as 'les derniers Frontenac'[2] and Yves is twice referred to as 'le dernier des Frontenac'.[3] Little wonder that Mauriac should have chosen the quotation from Rimbaud with which to prefix the second part of his novel:

> Que les oiseaux et les sources sont loin!
> Ca ne peut être que la fin du monde,
> en avançant.

Le Mystère Frontenac, however, not only describes the end of a magic childhood. Like the majority of Mauriac's novels it goes much further and marks the end of the family as a whole. In these terms then it is quite possible to consider *Le Mystère Frontenac* as being in no way essentially different from any of Mauriac's earlier works. Certainly it may lack some of the more extreme portrayals of particular human characteristics—Félicité's violent love for her son in *Génitrix* or the cloying overtones of incest in *Ce qui etait perdu*—but in mortal terms there is no more hope of survival for the Frontenac family than there is for any other, though like all of Mauriac's post 'conversion' novels *Le Mystère Frontenac* does contain the arbitrary imposition of a religious solution. The Frontenac family, it is suggested, are no ordinary mortals for they benefit from some form of divine approval, and throughout the novel there are references to them in suitable terms. José's sense of vocation is a 'sentiment religieux',[4] for Yves, Blanche, and Xavier are 'sacrés',[5] Xavier himself considers his nephews and nieces as 'ces petits êtres sacrés'[6] and willingly chants the 'paroles idiotes et sacrées'[7] which, by family tradition, accompany the carving of toy whistles. Most of all, it is Joséfa for whom the Frontenac family has this divine nature. Her devotion has all the attributes of a real cult,[8] and her affair with

[1] Ibid., p. 115.   [2] Ibid., p. 10.   [3] Ibid., p. 177 and p. 236.
[4] Ibid., p. 50.   [5] Ibid., p. 101.   [6] Ibid., p. 40.   [7] Ibid., p. 94.
[8] Ibid., p. 219.

Xavier is described as a fifteen-year-long sacrifice 'sur les autels de la divinité Frontenac'[1] of the 'demi-dieux'[2] whom she feels unworthy to approach.[3]

But such reactions as these are personal ones expressed internally within the dimension of the work by the characters, and an important step must be taken if we are to move beyond this and see the family as a group which is eternally united in the all embracing love of God. This is an external view imposed by Mauriac himself and he attempts to incorporate it into the novel through his portrayal of Yves.

In addition to projecting some of his own early life through Yves, Mauriac uses him as a witness. His choice to opt out of the society represented by his family enables him to look at it objectively, comment upon it and be a vehicle through which Mauriac can introduce a totally different attitude to life. Yet a literary career is clearly not Yves' real vocation; he has been singled out for greater work:

Tu es libre de traîner dans le monde un cœur que je n'ai pas créé pour le monde;—libre de chercher sur la terre une nourriture qui ne t'est pas destinée;—libre d'essayer d'assouvir une faim qui ne trouvera rien à sa mesure: toutes les créatures ne l'apaiseraient pas, et tu courras de l'une à l'autre. . . . [4]

Whether this be God, the voice of conscience, or delirium Yves chooses to ignore it; his religious practice suffers much to his mother's despair,[5] and his life of debauchery and pleasure in Paris seems to occupy his whole existence quite adequately. None the less it is Yves who, echoing Lacordaire, comforts Blanche with his certain faith in divine love: 'tout amour s'accomplirait dans l'unique Amour, (que) toute tendresse serait allégée et purifiée de ce qui l'alourdit et de ce qui la souille . . . '[6] and his life in Paris, punctuated as it is by moments of deep despair, is clearly not the literary haven that he had hoped to find. His true role in life is prefigured early in the novel in the allegory of the *fourmi-lion*. The common ant which is careless enough to stumble into the

---

[1] Ibid., p. 76.   [2] Ibid., p. 200.   [3] Ibid., p. 204.
[4] Ibid., p. 121.   [5] Ibid., p. 141.   [6] Ibid., p. 125.

trap is unable to escape no matter how hard it struggles, except through the intervention of a superior being—in this case Yves. Here Yves plays the part of God. In Paris the same idea is adopted once more, only on this occasion Yves is the ant, trapped in his own need to be loved in the same way that Jean-Louis had been enmeshed in the snare of the family business:

Et lui, Yves Frontenac, blessé, ensablé comme eux, mais créature libre et qui aurait pu s'arracher du monde, avait choisi de gémir en vain, confondu avec le reste de la forêt humaine.[1]

His only means of escape is his faith, and however bitter or despairing he may appear to become in the face of man's predicament his certain belief in God's beneficent love wins through in the end.

In this way Mauriac suggests that all is by no means lost and is able to endow the whole of the Frontenac family with special receptive qualities:

Le mystère Frontenac échappait à la destruction, car il était un rayon de l'éternel amour réfracté à travers une race. L'impossible union des époux, des frères et des fils serait consommée avant qu'il fût longtemps, et les derniers pins de Bourideys verraient passer—non plus à leurs pieds, dans l'allée qui va au gros chêne, mais très haut et très loin au-dessus de leurs cimes, le groupe éternellement serré de la mère et de ses cinq enfants.[2]

What is needed is the step of faith, the willingness to subordinate human love to divine love, for human relationships are, as he says in this closing sentence, impossible. The *mystère* of the Frontenac family is its special sense of communication not only within itself but with God: 'tout se passait chez les Frontenac, comme s'il y avait eu communication entre l'amour des frères et celui de la mère, ou comme si ces deux amours avaient eu une source unique'.[3] Yves and his brothers look back on their childhood as a time of innocence and purity, a time of family unity and peace, but no matter what values Mauriac should chose to put in childhood this view can only be a limited one. Luc and Marie in

[1] Ibid., p. 252.   [2] Ibid., p. 253.   [3] Ibid., p. 163.

Le Nœud de vipères also represent innocence and preserve it through their early deaths; in *Le Mystère Frontenac* death appears in its more usual role and Mauriac must go beyond it. This, as the bulk of the novel implies, requires an extra dimension but it is not worked into the pattern of the novel as a whole as is the notion of redemption in *Le Nœud de vipères* or *Les Anges noirs* for example. There is too much that is traditional Mauriac material in this novel for it to be an exception and even if we are able to accept the special nature of the Frontenac family this does not necessarily suggest that Mauriac succeeds in redressing his picture of humanity as a whole. When the novel first appeared Mauriac claimed that in many ways it was a reply to, and indeed a refutation of, Gide's celebrated comment. 'Familles, je vous hais.' But Gide's criticism of the family was of an institution which created particular social and moral obligations, and branded its members with certain stigma; Mauriac surely can not be said to linger far behind in such works as *Le Nœud de vipères* or *Préséances* even though his targets may be slightly narrower than Gide's. For the Catholic the family should represent the basic unit of society, a reflection in miniature of the family of the Church, but Mauriac's families can hardly be said to be exemplary and beneath their divine glow the Frontenacs are no exception. Louis de Mondadon saw the danger: 'Surtout n'allez pas mettre *Le Mystère Frontenac* dans les bibliothèques paroissiales!'[1] As a piece of advice, even for the Jesuit audience of *Etudes*, this may seem naïve, but it does indicate that Mauriac's attempt to project a religious solution into the novel is not convincing enough to compensate for the more traditional aspects of his writing. *Le Mystère Frontenac* remains very much in the 'grande voie' of Mauriac's imaginative writing and as Marcel Arland so rightly observed it falls easily into the pattern of all the post-conversion novels in particular: 'il [Mauriac] tende à chercher, à montrer sur la terre certaines traces d'un ciel qui l'a toujours hanté. C'est du moins ce qui me frappe dans son nouveau livre, plutôt qu'une simple apologie de la famille.'[2]

In order to write the exception that so many critics have seen in

[1] *Etudes*, 20 March 1933, p. 759.
[2] *Nouvelle Revue Française*, March 1933, p. 520.

Le Mystère Frontenac Mauriac was to wait another twenty years. When it appeared *L'Agneau* showed a marked change in both style and material, but its failure proved once and for all that Mauriac had long passed his most successful period of imaginative writing.

6

LATTER-DAY SAINTS

FOR some of his more enthusiastic supporters Mauriac's sudden silence as a novelist after the publication of *La Pharisienne* in 1941 was perhaps surprising, but Sartre's stringent criticism of *La Fin de la nuit* may have had a deeper effect on him than Mauriac has ever cared to admit, and the manner in which he is careful to exclude the author from *La Pharisienne* by a series of rather obvious devices certainly suggests this.[1] Mauriac's own explanation of the time lapse before the publication of *Le Sagouin* in 1951, however, is that he was otherwise fully committed:

Les travaux du journalisme politique m'ont absorbé, j'ai voulu également observer les nouveaux courants romanesques nés de la guerre, et surtout je ne sentais pas d'une façon impérieuse, le désir de m'embarquer à bord d'un roman.[2]

Certainly his participation during the war in the production of the clandestine paper *Les Lettres françaises* was both a dangerous and a full time occupation, but his imaginative writing had not been entirely neglected. *Le Sagouin*, originally intended for *La Table ronde*, had been abandoned 'surtout parce que le récit se perdait dans le sable et que ma femme, à qui je le dictais, ne trouvait pas cela bon'.[3] Later when asked to write a *nouvelle* Mauriac fortunately found the forgotten manuscript, and when it eventually appeared the work impressed many by its brevity and bleakness of style, recalling Mauriac's writing of the early twenties. But in spite of such illustrious forebears as *Le Baiser au lépreux*, *Génitrix*, and *Thérèse Desqueyroux* with which it has perhaps most in common, *Le Sagouin* fails to communicate the

[1] C. C. O'Brien, p. 35, also makes this point.
[2] 'Ce que sera le prochain roman de François Mauriac', *Figaro littéraire*, 31 January 1948, p. 1.
[3] *Figaro littéraire*, 25 February 1956, p. 1.

same intensity. As we have already noticed in Chapter Three, standard themes link the book to the main body of Mauriac's work—archaic bourgeois aspirations, dying religious faith, the failure of human marriage, and in particular an inevitable movement towards physical degeneration and death. But there is no single dominating point of focus and Paule's mental outrage but wholly ineffectual revolt is flimsy material indeed compared with the attempted poisoning of a husband. Aware of this perhaps, Mauriac seems to do his best to ensure that Paule does not enjoy the sympathy that was so readily given to Thérèse. The provincial intellectual has gone, replaced by an insipid and insignificant orphan. The 'front vaste' which even when worn by age dazzled Georges Filhot in *La Fin de la nuit* gives way to 'un front étroit, mal délimité'.[1] Paule's clothes are stained and untidy, and she is almost an alcoholic.[2] The fatal charm which dogged Thérèse like an evil spirit and which caused others to be irrisistibly attracted to her is reversed in Paule into a simple feeling of sympathy for the oppressed because she convinces herself that their predicament is similar to her own. While this sympathy can win over the young priest, it has no real attraction for the happily married and successful *instituteur*, Robert Bordas. There is also a feeble echo of *Génitrix* in the relationship between mother and daughter-in-law, but their petty squabbles entirely lack the intensity of Félicité Cazenave's hatred for Mathilde. In spite of these and other affinities with earlier novels, *Le Sagouin* hardly bears comparison, but it does contain a new element in the double death of Galéas and his son. Unlike some earlier works *Le Sagouin* does not posit a solution to the problem of redemption nor does it explore the influence of Grace in the present. In their place through his description of this shared death, the search for what Bordas describes as 'ce royaume des esprits' Mauriac is setting faith in a future life in which the unloved and the misunderstood of this world will find respite. This theme reappears and is extended in Mauriac's next novel, *Galigaï*, and is eventually given much fuller expression in *L'Agneau*.

Like *Le Sagouin*, *Galigaï* has certain obvious affinities with earlier novels. The central theme is apparently that of family

[1] S, p. 9.   [2] Ibid., pp. 41 and 42.

opposition to the marriage between Marie Dubernet and Gilles Salone. On behalf of Marie, Galigaï assumes the task of overcoming this opposition, though not without the hope of some personal benefit. A frustrated spinster herself,[1] she hopes that her complicity will be rewarded by marriage to Gilles' friend Nicolas Plassac, and it is her indomitable will power—'Heureusement j'ai de la volonté pour deux'[2]—which drives her on. Ironically she loses her prey and instead marries her former employer Armand Dubernet almost immediately after his wife's death, and in doing so herself falls victim to the social machine. Dubernet is satisfied not because he has finally caught a woman who has always fascinated him, but primarily because he has acquired more property: 'il allait épouser l'héritière de Belmonte, il posséderait Agathe, Belmonte serait à lui'.[3] Once more in this novel Mauriac explores the relationship between a mother and her son as Nicolas Plassac moves from complete submission to the wishes and blindness to the faults of his mother, through revolt forced upon him by the attentions of Galigaï, to freedom. As in *Le Sagouin*, however, the absence of any central crisis makes for a diffuse and untidy action. There are too many points of interest and, as in all of Mauriac's early novels, a series of sub plots involving pairs of characters. Moreover Julie Dubernet, Armand's first wife, is present for most of the book, recalling Mauriac's traditional pious middle-aged women who attempt to ensure their eternal bliss by charitable works on earth.

However, the intricate pattern of provincial life in Dorthe, especially as it is worked out between the four principal characters and dominated by the figure of Galigaï herself, is only intended as a background to what Mauriac confesses to be his real purpose: 'Le monde que je décris est tel que le découvrent les yeux dessillés de Nicolas.'[4] Here the connection can be made with *Le Sagouin*. Nicolas Plassac rejects life in much the same way as Galéas and Guillaume had done in an attempt to discover the eternal kingdom of God. At the close of the novel he faces life anew: 'Étranger à lui-même, détaché de toute créature, il s'assit sur le

---

[1] There are in this novel as in *TD* faint suggestions of lesbianism: see for example p. 26 and p. 79.

[2] *GAL*, p. 129.   [3] Ibid., p. 157.   [4] Ibid., p. 169.

parapet et il demeurait là comme s'il avait donné rendez-vous à
quelqu'un',[1] and to ensure that this is not misinterpreted Mauriac
informs his reader in the *Postface* that 'ce "quelqu'un" qui
attend Nicolas Plassac [. . .] c'est Dieu'.[2] Yet between this novel
and *Le Sagouin* there is an important difference. For Galéas and
his son the attempt to find a life of love and compassion was
motivated by personal despair, and they plunge into the unknown
with no assurance that they will discover God. The step they take
demands death and is the result of their having been rejected by
this world. Nicolas too has, in a sense, been rejected, but his
detachment is motivated more by personal choice, and he remains alive believing that God can be best served in this world.
In this way Nicolas Plassac heralds the significant appearance in
L'Agneau of Mauriac's lay saint, Xavier Dartigelongue.

Unlike the majority of his other novels which were written
with considerable ease and speed, *L'Agneau* was produced slowly
and with difficulty. On 3 April 1954 Mauriac wrote in a *bloc-note*:
'J'ai rapetassé le roman que je traîne depuis plusieurs années',[3] and
a week later:

Hier, j'ai apporté moi-même, chez Flammarion, le manuscrit de
L'Agneau. Depuis plusieurs années que je l'oublie, que je le retrouve,
que je l'allège de chapitres entiers, que j'en invente d'autres, il faut être
un spécialiste de manuscrits, comme le directeur littéraire de la maison,
pour s'y reconnaître. Cet *Agneau* avait fait si peur à la revue qui devait
d'abord le publier que, pris moi-même de panique, je l'avais jeté aux
oubliettes. Mais il ne s'y laissait pas oublier. Un manuscrit, cela bouge:
comme quand une femme grosse dit: 'Il remue'. Voici donc *l'Agneau*
encore gluant sur ses hautes pattes mal assurées. Je l'ai léché, reléché
et pourléché avant de le jeter sur la table de l'éditeur qui l'a emporté
dans une serviette.[4]

The difficulty which Mauriac experienced results above all from
the subject of the work. He had originally set out to write the life
of a saint but found that 'un autre protagoniste, personnage

---

[1] Ibid., p. 164.   [2] Ibid., p. 169.

[3] *B-N*, p. 69. Chapter I of the first draft was probably written at Malagar a year
or two after the liberation. See *Figaro littéraire*, 25 February 1956, p. 1. In the
manuscripts reference is made to 1948.

[4] Ibid., p. 72.

luciférien et plus qu'inquiétant, s'était poussé sous le projecteur. Mon travail a donc consisté surtout à régler l'éclairage.'[1] If we are to judge from Mauriac's own comments about this work—and he shows more uncertainty about this than any other—and from critical reactions, it was this very attempt to explore new material which caused the novel's relative failure.

In a pre-publication interview with Pierre Mazars, Mauriac, without actually defining Xavier as a saint, pointed out that his fate was to 'souffrir à la place des autres et mourir par et pour les autres'.[2] This 'vocation du malheur' as he also defined it, was soon seized by critics as the crucial point of the book. André Billy in a very favourable review remarked that 'Ce saint [Xavier] est aussi un faible. Son besoin d'amour le perdra.'[3] Other critics were not wholly convinced that Xavier's capacity for self sacrifice counterbalanced the evil projected into the novel through Jean de Mirbel, while André Wurmser maintained that the work was completely unreal, was peopled with monsters and was 'pénible, étouffant, limité aux mauvaises odeurs des âmes et des peaux'.[4] Even André Rousseaux in a relatively inoffensive review decided that, more than any other Mauriac novel, L'Agneau showed that love between mortals is impossible and that it was yet another portrait of 'ce monde affreux qui n'a que le surnatural pour revanche et consolation'.[5]

On the other hand André Blanchet, reviewing the novel at some length for Etudes, compared Mauriac's achievement in writing L'Agneau with Racine and Phèdre. It was, he maintained, Mauriac's masterpiece towards which all his earlier work had been moving: 'Mauriac s'est longtemps cherché, il s'est enfin trouvé.'[6] However much he may have tried in his earlier work, Blanchet continues, Mauriac had been unable to inject the theme of the influence of Grace into his world of human passion; there had always been a clearly defined division between the two. Now for the first time the problem essential to all Catholic novelists has been overcome—the involvement of Grace as the very core of a work and at the same time the avoidance of all didacticism:

[1] Ibid., p. 69. [2] Figaro littéraire, 1 June 1954, p. 1.
[3] Le Figaro, 30 June 1954, p. 13. [4] Les Lettres françaises, 8–15 July 1954, p. 5.
[5] Figaro littéraire, 3 July 1954, p. 2. [6] Op. cit., September, 1954, p. 263.

Autre inconvénient de cette intervention tardive de Dieu: le monde des passions humaines constituait un théâtre trop bien clos pour admettre d'autres acteurs que les siens. La grâce n'y pouvait agir que du dehors, par effraction. Survenant au terme d'un roman de Mauriac, toute conversion risquait fort de paraître invraisemblable, parce que cette conclusion sacrée n'était pas précontenue dans les données premières, toutes profanes. Il semblait alors que l'on voulut tirer frauduleusement le plus du moins.

Il n'est sans doute pour l'artiste qu'un moyen de rendre plausible une conversion, c'est de nous plonger d'entrée de jeu dans le jeu divin, c'est installer Dieu au plein centre de l'œuvre comme il est est au centre du monde, c'est d'en faire l'acteur principal de toute tragédie humaine.[1]

In this passage Blanchet does little more than summarize the common-places of hostile critical reaction to Mauriac's writing. At the same time his suggestion that *L'Agneau* fulfils the requirements of the Catholic novel precisely because it introduces Grace as an active participant must remain debatable. Blanchet's interpretation demands the same degree of faith as does Charles du Bos' analysis of the problem of the Catholic novel, and Mauriac's own discussion of it in *Le Romancier et ses personnages*; it may be a satisfactory answer for the believer who already accepts that even in the murkiest of human dramas the divine presence is ultimately visible, but it will not necessarily convince nor be acceptable to the non-believer. Moreover, Mauriac's own doubts on the general balance of the work are hardly an incentive for us to accept Blanchet's judgement unquestioningly. We are faced in *L'Agneau*, as we are in *Le Mystère Frontenac*, with the problem of involving Mauriac's intention with the limiting, traditional features of his writing. In the later novel the two are certainly more easily separable, but Mauriac veers much more closely towards didacticism and overt moralizing with, as he has admitted, little success.

In *L'Agneau* Mauriac has reduced unnecessary description to a minimum, allowing the action to be conveyed for the most part through a series of conversations and through Xavier's own reflections. The novel is divided into three sections each of which is an elaborate flashback much in the manner of *Le Désert de*

[1] *Etudes*, p. 266.

l'amour, having its starting point in a conversation between Jean de Mirbel and his wife Michèle during one sleepless night when they confess their mutual responsibility for Xavier's death. Factually the plot is simple. Xavier Dartigelongue, an unsettled, middle-class young man decides, after two attempts at other careers, to enter a Carmelite seminary in Paris. On the journey he meets Jean de Mirbel who persuades him that he alone can reconcile him with his wife. Xavier who, in spite of warnings to the contrary from his *directeur de conscience*, believes that all those he meets have need of his love is an easy prey and he returns to the Mirbel house at Larjuzon. Here he is influenced by three people in particular: Dominique, the young girl who is acting as a temporary secretary for Brigitte Pian, Michèle's mother; Roland, an orphan adopted for a trial period by the childless Mirbel couple; and the curé de Baluzac. Typically Xavier feels that he has been called to play an important and necessary part in the lives of all three, and this he attempts to do with varying degrees of success until he meets his death in an accident with a car driven by Jean.

Such factual simplicity, however, is overlain not only with religious allegory but also with a thoroughly unnatural setting; as André Wurmser wrote, Mauriac has peopled this novel with abnormal beings and suggestions. Jean is clearly impotent in the presence of his wife,[1] and hints of homosexuality[2] and a general obsession with sex are to be found everywhere.[3] It is of course important that throughout the novel, Xavier, like Alain Forcas in *Les Anges noirs*, is seen as an ordinary young man: 'Il était un garçon comme tous les garçons.'[4] He is evidently uncertain about training for the priesthood and, more importantly, he is sufficiently human to be physically attracted to Dominique. Mauriac is aware of the danger of creating in Xavier an exemplary figure totally devoid of human emotions and hence quite unreal, yet it may also be argued that on more than one occasion such an awareness has resulted in distortion.

[1] See, for example, *A*, pp. 63, 74, 149.
[2] See, for example, ibid., pp. 8–9, 84, 105, 108, 150.
[3] See, for example, ibid., pp. 99, 116, 144.
[4] Ibid., p. 142. Cf. p. 48.

As the title suggests Xavier assumes the responsibility for all
those who enter his life even to the point of sacrifice. Analogies
with Christ and His suffering are discussed at almost every turn
especially the episode in Chapters Eight and Nine which describes
Xavier's nocturnal visit to Roland, Michèle's discovery of the
blood stains the following morning and her subsequent care for
him. Yet these are obvious analogies and, while many of Xavier's
actions are indeed Christlike, on a number of occasions trans-
figuration is complete. During this same episode, for example,
the vision which Xavier has of Christ occurs as a climax and in
turn forces the reader to consider Xavier as Christ in person.

Dans une tension atroce, il avançait, et croyait voir bouger devant lui
un dos maigre; il en discernait les vertèbres, les côtes soulevées par un
halètement précipité, et le sillon violet des vieilles flagellations: l'esclave
de tous les temps, l'esclave éternel.[1]

On several other occasions the change occurs more subtly. At the
end of the section which precedes the scene of the Cross, Xavier
is discovered praying alone just as Christ had prayed before His
crucifixion; when he visits the Curé de Baluzac Xavier senses for
a brief moment that he is no longer himself: 'Alors Xavier avait
prononcé cette parole absurde (l'avait-il réellement prononcée?):
"Je suis là, pourtant. Je suis venu." '[2] He must also face a series of
temptations: an intellectual one to which he succumbs when he
allows Jean to persuade him to return to Larjuzon, a sensual one
personified principally by Dominique but also by Michèle, and
finally the temptation to abuse the power of free choice by
deliberately turning his back on God. It is this third temptation,
coming as it does from a priest, which convinces Xavier of the
unwillingness of the human race to recognize Christ at any time
and which makes him realize the true nature of his love for others.

In an answer to André Rousseaux's review of *L'Agneau* Mauriac
maintains that the essential pages of the book are given to the
account of the love shared by Dominique and Xavier. Inasmuch
as this relationship creates a tension within Xavier's mind this is
acceptable enough but, Mauriac continues, Xavier 'aimant
Dominique, croit qu'une permission de bonheur va lui être

---

[1] Ibid., p. 166.   [2] Ibid., pp. 208–9.

accordée enfin ... '[1] and that this hope is destroyed by the blinding revelation of divine love. Were this love to have the intensity and the hold on Xavier that Mauriac claims the result would indeed be tragic and Rousseaux justified in accusing Mauriac of having written yet another chapter in 'le désert de l'amour'. But it does not. No matter how Mauriac may have attempted to make Xavier appear 'comme tous les garçons', in the reader's eyes at least he shrinks from a love that will make demands of his body. What he seeks instead is a spiritual union and he deliberately rejects the possibility of earthly happiness with Dominique in order to fulfil his role as a redeemer for mankind, and such a decision, as it did for Christ, entails witting self-sacrifice. The accident in which Xavier meets his death is his crucifixion and Jean who drives the car represents the human race which sacrificed Christ nearly two thousand years before. Over all lies the bitter irony that man has not learned his lesson; even the mediocre curé de Baluzac will continue to sacrifice Christ[2] and prefer mortal love with its attendant suffering to the infinitely more rewarding union with God. Yet even this is not total despair. By his infinite capacity for redemption Christ will ultimately overcome evil; Jean and Michèle awaken to an 'aube glacée' but it is a dawn none the less.

The significance of L'Agneau is twofold. On the one hand it is a statement about man's unwillingness to accept Christ, but more importantly it is an extension of the search for God undertaken by Galéas and Guillaume de Cernès in Le Sagouin and by Nicolas Plassac in Galigaï. L'Agneau describes a religious vocation, and by insisting as he does on the ordinariness of Xavier, Mauriac is attempting to show that the same capacity for love and even self-sacrifice exists in all men if they can bring themselves to admit it. In this sense the case of Xavier Dartigelongue represents, as Blanchet suggested, a logical extension to the whole of Mauriac's work. He has attempted to write a novel which convinces us of the redemptive power of Christ's love for man, but by its very nature the novel presents an extreme case, an ideal, and no matter how Mauriac strives to modify this by emphasizing the essentially human context from which it springs he is unable to convince us.

[1] B-N, p. 113.   [2] Ibid., p. 242.

His eagerness to prove the necessity and efficacy of religious faith through the medium of his imaginative writing cannot be left without a brief consideration of his film scenario, *Le Pain vivant*, which appeared a year after *L'Agneau* in 1955. In the *Préface* to this work Mauriac somewhat glibly denies the didactic overtones of *L'Agneau*:

J'ai raconté beaucoup d'histoires depuis un demi-siècle que j'écris. C'est pourtant la première fois que j'en invente une avec l'intention de prouver quelque chose. Non que je n'aie défendu ma foi, mais ce fut dans des articles, dans des essais. Aucun de mes romans n'a été conçu avec des arrière-pensées de prédication. Ce qu'il y transparaît d'inquiétude religieuse ou de ferveur se trouve là malgré moi, et parce qu'au fruit on reconnaît l'arbre.[1]

Le Pain vivant is, to be sure, much more overtly didactic than *L'Agneau*, but the similarity of theme and even perhaps the fact that according to the manuscripts the film was at first to be entitled *Le Sang qu'on ne voit pas* suggests that Mauriac is not being absolutely honest.

As a film *Le Pain vivant* was a total failure, but in retrospect Mauriac still refers to it with some regret and maintains that with a more experienced producer it would have combined an extensive cinematic appeal with a profound religious significance. One wonders, however, if Mauriac's faith in his own work is not being severely tested. The plot is so contrived that it is not difficult to predict its development from the opening scenes. Thérèse Valmont is the last of Mauriac's 'filles dévotes' whose natural inclinations like Xavier's are opposed and often completely suppressed by her sense of religious (and hence moral) duty. Her self-appointed task in life is to care for her father and her brother Luc. The former, abandoned by his wife, allows a possessive love for Thérèse to be distorted by jealousy; the latter whose legitimacy is in doubt redeems an otherwise dissipated nature through his love for his sister. Thérèse falls in love with Valmy, a student and the agnostic son of an *instituteur*. Despite her tentative efforts to renounce him she eventually succumbs to his offers of love and marriage, though her mission is not entirely lost since she converts him to Roman

[1] Op. cit., p. 5.

Catholicism. The final scene in the film which takes place at La Salette offers some of the most obvious symbolism to be found in Mauriac's work. Grasping the cross with one hand Valmy prevents Thérèse from flinging herself over the cliff: 'Cette main de Valmy qui agrippe la croix, c'est comme un trait d'union entre la croix et elle.'[1] Echoes of *L'Agneau* are heard throughout. Thérèse for example remarks to Valmy: 'Je ne crois pas aux coincidences, je ne crois pas au hasard. Ce n'est pas par hasard que mon frère a surgi juste au moment où je vous parlais de la croix qui se dresse dans chacune de nos vies.'[2] She plays on the equivocal sense of *abandonner*: 'quoi qu'il advienne, je ne vous abandonnerai jamais [. . .] Je vous le promets toujours . . . Je serai avec vous, à tous les instants de votre vie, sans vous voir, sans vous entendre. J'y serai encore alors que, depuis des années, vous ne penserez plus à moi . . . '.[3]

Even though on Mauriac's own admission *Le Pain vivant* goes a stage further than *L'Agneau* in its presentation of a personal belief, there remains a common problem. Together these works move in a new direction, but the difficulties which Mauriac experienced over the actual writing of *L'Agneau* reflect his inability to escape totally from the type of novel he had written before and the failure of both works indicates the futility of his attempt. Mauriac's most successful presentation of Catholicism lay in the novels written some twenty years earlier when the traditional features of his writing were gradually shaped to accommodate a religious message. Mauriac may be entirely justified when he remarks that *L'Agneau* is 'le livre le plus vrai que j'aie écrit';[4] unfortunately what he has to say conflicts with his means of saying it. Both *L'Agneau* and *Le Pain vivant* smack too much of a thesis to be convincing imaginative literature, and on this evidence one can only agree with what Bernanos and Mauriac himself had said in the mid-twenties.

[1] *PV*, p. 165. [2] Ibid., p. 67.
[3] Ibid., p. 70 and p. 94. [4] *B-N*, p. 273.

CONCLUSION

IN spite of the appearance during recent years of an increasing number of Mauriac titles in the *Livre de poche* collection, few would disagree that his reputation as a novelist is less widespread than it was before the last World War, and even his recent decision to try his hand at novel writing again after fourteen years is unlikely to alter this situation radically. On the other hand Mauriac's choosing to deposit his manuscripts in the care of the Fonds Doucet in Paris will almost certainly mark the beginning of a new scholarly interest in his work, and we shall surely see before long detailed critical editions of individual works together with the kind of exhaustive study which carefully traces the influences and sources of his immense production. What I have attempted in this book is far less ambitious but, I hope, none the less useful. As I have indicated Mauriac's reputation as a Catholic novelist involves a certain notion which has never been adequately explained either in terms of his own writing or in terms of French literature as a whole. Indeed a valuable contribution to the study of modern French literature and even modern European literature would be an analysis of a number of novels all of which have at some time been defined as Catholic in order to discover what it is that they have in common. Perhaps the only factor which permits this definition is the personal faith of the authors concerned, and as we saw in the *Introduction* even this would be a position that was hard to defend. Fortunately for the moment this problem does not arise. As far as Mauriac is concerned the reality of his faith has never been in doubt in spite of the crisis of the 1920s, but his ability to see beyond his personal position in order to incorporate it in or to project it into the public statement of a novel has not always been realized as successfully as he would have liked. Indeed, as I have tried to show, only *Le Nœud de vipères* and *Les Anges noirs* emerge as novels in which the religious element forms an integral part of the action and structure. In this way Mauriac's achievement may be said to be limited and to fall well short of his intention, but his consciousness of the problems involved has led to a series of novels which, while limited in many respects, offer an interesting and worthwhile subject for study.

POSTSCRIPT

Un Adolescent d'autrefois[1]

'Ecrire c'est se souvenir . . .' François Mauriac

IN deciding to write a new novel some fourteen years after the publication of *L'Agneau*, Mauriac has at last effected his claim that he could always write another work of fiction should he ever decide to do so. Renewed practice, however, has not brought with is any noticeable change in his selection of material. In *Un Adolescent d'autrefois* Mauriac has, predictably enough and as the title suggests, returned for his material to the well-known world of Bordeaux and the *landes* of his early years at the turn of the century. Like many of his earlier novels the plot is deceptively simple. Written in the form first of a diary and later as an account of events for his friend André Donzac, *Un Adolescent d'autrefois* is the story of five years in the life of a young man, Alain Gajac. The greater part of this time is spent either on his family's estates at Maltaverne or in Bordeaux where he is a student; at the end of the novel he moves to Paris ostensibly to embark on research. Alain and his elder brother Laurent, who dies of tuberculosis at an early age, are brought up by a widowed and possessive mother. When he moves to Bordeaux Alain meets and falls in love with Marie, a girl eight years older than himself who works in a book shop and whose background is totally incompatible with his own. His mother, for whom any resultant marriage would be socially quite unacceptable, sees this affair as a threat both to her personal

---

[1] Only after the completion of this book was Mauriac's most recent novel, *Un Adolescent d'autrefois* published, and I am grateful to the Clarendon Press for allowing me at this late stage to consider it in this brief *Postscript*. Mauriac is also under contract to write two further novels which, if his previous rate of production is maintained, will no doubt appear in as many years. From the evidence of *Un Adolescent d'autrefois*, however, and from what Mauriac himself has said, it seems unlikely that there will be any radical change in his work.

relationship with her son and to her plans for the management of their family property. Her aim is for Alain to marry Jeannette Séris, the daughter of a distant cousin and neighbour, Numa Séris, for in this way as sole heirs they would unite the properties of the two most influential and wealthy landowners of the district. Alain who is filled with horror at the idea of such an arranged marriage and who has a physical loathing for the young girl (cruelly nicknamed Le Pou), finds in Marie the chance to escape, and he is encouraged in his plans to do so by Simon Duberc, the son of his mother's estate manager. Simon who sees the only outlet for his petty ambitions in the church is temporarily won over by the local atheist mayor, Monsieur Duport, and it is during this period of waywardness that he assumes the role of confidant and conspirator for both Alain and Marie. When the time comes for Alain to effect his escape by announcing his engagement to Marie he discovers that not only does his mother react much more vigorously than they had anticipated, but that his own family ties are too strong. He returns to Maltaverne where one day he happens by chance to discover Jeannette bathing. At first he fails to recognize her so attracted is he by her youth and freshness. He follows her through the woods but a dry twig which snaps underfoot draws her attention to him and she runs away, but only, as Alain discovers hours later, to her death; she is strangled by a local farm worker. While Alain holds himself at least in part responsible for her death it also has a beneficial effect in that it breaks the spell that Maltaverne has had over him. He mourns her, realizing now that it is too late that he did in fact love her. He leaves his home and Bordeaux for Paris where his life, initially, is uneventful. As the book closes it is suggested that he is on the point of forming a new liaison with a girl (possibly a prostitute) who comes regularly to the restaurant he frequents.

This is the barest and most superficial summary of the plot, but it is enough to suggest that Mauriac has returned to a number of standard themes: marriages of convenience, family disputes, a desire for wealth and social status, and an interpretation of religious values that is totally false.[1] Moreover as in so many of

[1] See, for example, *AA*, p. 8, p. 19 and pp. 55–6.

his novels he has also introduced a number of thinly disguised autobiographical details of varying significance: the time sequence (1902–7) exactly coincides with Mauriac's own early years, while Alain's scholarly achievements and intentions even to the extent of writing a thesis on the history of the Franciscan movement in France are also Mauriac's own. In André Donzac we have a direct representation of André Lacaze from whom Mauriac learned about modernism,[1] Keller the social catholic student who is a member of Sangnier's *Sillon* has clear affinities with Philippe Borrell;[2] Laurent's death from tuberculosis recalls that of Mauriac's own cousin Raymond Laurens.[3] Even the family properties at Maltaverne and the apartments in the rue de Cheverus in Bordeaux or the rue Vaugirard in Paris are taken directly from his personal memories. Noticeable too is the way in which *Un Adolescent d'autrefois* is an amalgam of a large number of characters, episodes and themes which have already made their appearance in different guises in earlier works: memories of Louis of *Le Nœud de vipères* and Desbats of *Les Anges noirs* are revived by the 'vieux de Lassus';[4] Gabriel Gradère is recalled by Alain himself, 'moitié-démon, moitié-ange',[5] and the Du Buch sisters by the demoiselles de Jouanhaut with whom Alain stays when his brother is taken ill.[6] Alain's words to his anxious mother on his departure for Paris—'Je crois que toutes nos rencontres, mêmes les pires, sont voulues'[7]—recall those of Xavier in *L'Agneau* or of Thérèse in *Le Pain vivant*. Similarly Alain's account of his mother's view of sexual love and marriage strongly echoes Mme Duprouy's advice to her daughters in *Le Rang*.[8] All of these features and many more besides make it quite clear that in substance at least there has been

[1] NMI, pp. 146–50, NB-N (1961–4), p. 103 and pp. 450–1.
[2] MI, pp. 31–2. Borrell may also be the person behind the portrait of Vincent Hiéron in ECC.
[3] NMI, p. 233.
[4] AA, p. 84. 'et si lentement que j'avance, je finirais par devenir pareil au vieux de Lassus avec mes trois mille hectares et une meute d'héritiers qui me harcèleraient, que je haïrais, que je tiendrais comme lui à distance'.
[5] Ibid., p. 59.
[6] Cf. NMI, pp. 58–61.
[7] AA, p. 245. See above, p. 105.
[8] Ibid., pp. 105–6.

no radical change of policy, a point that the novel's immediate reviewers were quick to make.[1]

In view of this, therefore, it is not unreasonable to attempt to evaluate *Un Adolescent d'autrefois* in terms of Mauriac's earlier novels. At once certain improvements are evident particularly his greater control in the handling of the central issues of the mother-son relationship and of the intrigues of Alain, Marie, and Simon. In addition the treatment of secondary themes, so fragmentary in the early novels, is here much tidier. There are, however, some exceptions. The relationship between Simon and Mme Duport for example appears to serve no purpose beyond that of having a mildly scandalous nature which provokes certain social and moral indignations in the Gajac household, and even Simon's being temporarily dissuaded from the priesthood by Monsieur Duport is not relevant to his major role in the book. Similarly the 'vieux de Lassus' and the problems which confront him over the inheritance of his property only seem to be included as a particularly sharp illustration of a regular Mauriac theme. Why too should we be informed of Alain's undeclared adolescent passion for Mlle Martineau, who appears briefly on one occasion only, unless through the idealized description of her as Joan of Arc Mauriac is deliberately drawing a comparison with the suggestion of a prostitute at the close of the book in order to indicate the extent to which Alain has shed his inhibitions and illusions?[2] Yet while these may indeed appear to be unfinished or even irrelevant incidents, by writing this novel partly in the form of a diary and partly as a series of recollections, Mauriac is able, legitimately, to introduce them.

The real achievement of *Un Adolescent d'autrefois*, however, lies in Mauriac's treatment of the mother-son relationship and in his consideration of the problem of human communication. The first of these themes is one which regularly makes its appearance throughout his work from *Génitrix* and *Le Mal* to *Galigaï* and *L'Agneau*. Together with Félicité Cazenave and even Blanche

---

[1] Jean Freustie, for example, in the *Nouvel Observateur*, 10–16 March 1969, p. 50, writes that *AA* provides us with 'la vingtième mouture d'un thème que nous connaissons par cœur'.

[2] *AA*, p. 32 and p. 266.

Frontenac, Mme Gajac is primarily a business woman who visualizes and evaluates her life in the narrow and limited terms of material possession and social prestige, remaining quite indifferent to Alain's academic and literary tastes: 'Elle m'aime, mais je ne l'intéresse pas. Rien ne l'intéresse que les propriétés.'[1] The death of Laurent, who like José Frontenac had been the 'paysan de la famille', makes her even more determined to ensure that the family estates will not be dispersed after her death, and she attempts to arrange Alain's marriage for him: 'Elle me préférait infiniment le bonheur de régner, vieille régente, sur le royaume de son fils—et ce fils, elle l'immolait d'avance, elle l'avait déjà immoleé en pensée, en l'accouplant au Pou, sans excuse, sans même l'excuse d'ignorer ce qu'est l'amoux des corps.'[2] This at least is how Alain, who it must be remembered is narrating the story, views her designs. Similarly her vigilant care when he announces his engagement to Marie is interpreted by him as having been prompted by the same reason. Indeed through Alain's descriptions of her Madame Gajac emerges as a much less sympathetic figure than Blanche Frontenac with whom in view of the noticeable parallel between Alain's life and Mauriac's own early years comparison is inevitably invited. Only towards the end of the book does Alain come to realize his mistaken interpretation and the real reason for his mother's wish that he should marry Jeannette. For her this young girl represents the real child of the society to which she belongs. With the death of Laurent the only one of her children to whom she could turn for undertanding had gone; in Jeannette she sought a substitute:

Oui, je le voyais enfin: une vieille femme avait déversé sur une petite fille toute la tendresse dont personne au long de sa vie ne s'était soucié sinon un mari qui sans doute lui faisait physiquement horreur, sinon moi, mais je lui demeurais intelligible, d'une autre race, bien que je fusse sorti d'elle; j'approfondissais par ma seule présence le gouffre de solitude dans lequel la pauvre 'madame' se serait enfoncée sans

---

[1] Ibid., p. 13, cf. p. 80. 'Elle adorait la terre, mais pas à ma manière, elle haïssait les partages. . . .'
[2] Ibid., p. 109.

les propriétés qui la maintenaient à la surface, sans les dévotions qui
jalonnaient ses journées. . . . Mais il y a eu cette enfant que je haïssais,
et qui m'aimait, et qu'elle aima.[1]

The fact that Alain takes so long to realize that he is guilty of
this misinterpretation underlines the problem of communication
to which Mauriac so frequently returns. As in *Le Désert de l'amour*,
for example, where Maria Cross is viewed in various ways by a
number of different people or even in *Le Nœud de vipères* where
Louis' real nature remains hidden to all but Janine, each of the
main characters in *Un Adolescent d'autrefois* is only incompletely
understood by any other. Marie both hides facts about her past
life from Alain and lies about the present; her account of her
conversation in the book shop with Madame Gajac for example is,
according to the latter's subsequent version at least, quite untrue[2]
and it is only through her confessions to Simon, who maliciously
betrays her to Alain that he becomes aware of the extent to which
she is prepared to deceive him. Each of the characters in the novel
creates an imagined world in which to seek refuge or consolation;
Madame Gajac in her hopes of a marriage between Alain and
Jeannette; Simon in his plans to make himself indispensable to
Alain once he has returned to Maltaverne with Marie as his wife;
Marie in her aim to defeat Madame Gajac by seducing Alain
from the possessive mother love of which she believes him to be
a victim. Of them all, however, it is Alain who most consistantly
hides from reality. Religion, nature, physical love and literature
all in turn have the same function. In particular he discovers (as
did Mauriac at the same age) that religious faith and the natural
world blend together:

Le vent était tiède, une haleine, comme les poètes écrivent par habi-
tude, mais ce jour-là, le cliché était vrai: une haleine, le souffle d'un être
vivant. J'avais cru me moquer du Doyen, or cette moquerie, je
découvrais qu'elle m'avait non certes délivré, mais rendu conscient d'un
amour qui demeurait mon refuge de tous les instants. Adoration qui
n'avait jamais empiété sur l'autre amour, sur l'autre adoration que je

[1] Ibid., pp. 236–7, cf. p. 232, 'Je l'aimais cette petite fille, comme je n'ai jamais
aimé personne, pas même toi.'
[2] Ibid., pp. 198–203 and pp. 206–7.

vouais au Dieu chrétien, confondu avec le pain et avec le vin qui sont nés de la terre, du soleil et des pluies. Ce n'était pas trop de ce double refuge. Je n'aurais jamais trop de refuges contre les hommes.[1]

In Bordeaux the cathedral serves the same purpose: 'C'était l'endroit du monde où je me sentais le plus à l'abri du monde et comme immergé dans cet amour sans rivage dout j'étais séparé à jamais, moi le jeune homme riche "qui s'éloigna triste parce qu'il avait de grands biens".'[2] So too does Marie: 'il [Alain] se blottissait contre elle, il se faisait bercer'.[3] In essence Alain is a child, and whatever his personal ambitions may be he is never able to achieve complete emancipation.[4] In the same way as Jean Péloueyre in *Le Baiser au lépreux* is attracted to Nietzsche, Alain delights in evoking certain of Balzac's characters precisely because they are the personifications of the strong personality which he will never possess himself. He remains to the end of the novel not only stamped by his sheltered upbringing but also by his particular obsessions. In spite of his relationship with Marie the question of sex and physical love, the touchstone of morality for his mother, haunts Alain as well and induces in him a permanent sense of guilt.

From this it is possible to see that not only has Mauriac been unwilling (or unable) to change his material, but also his manipulation of it. Alain Gajac is yet another of Mauriac's young men whose lives lack both stability and direction; he has much in common with both Jean-Paul Johanet and Yves Frontenac, and it is remarkable that Mauriac can turn to his own early years once again with such accuracy and powers of evocation. But he has come no nearer to solving the problem of the Catholic novel. Certainly religious faith is an important element in the book but, intuitively recognized by Alain only, it is never worked into the fabric of the novel as a whole as it is in *Le Nœud de vipères* for

[1] Ibid., pp. 28–9.
[2] Ibid., p. 145.
[3] Ibid., p. 152.
[4] In an interview granted to Pierre Dumayet for *Le Monde*, Mauriac remarked: 'Alain est de ces garçons qui transforment toutes les femmes en mère' (*Le Monde, Supplément au numéro 7517*, 15 March 1969, p. v).

example.[1] Moreover when Alain comforts his mother as she questions the justice of a God who can allow an innocent young girl to be brutally raped and murdered, his words are out of character; it is as though Mauriac the novelist and convinced Catholic is speaking for him,[2] and the illusion created by the first person narrative is momentarily destroyed. It is, however, in his handling of this immense perspective in time that the real merit of Un Adolescent d'autrefois lies. In spite of its many similarities with other novels it is possible that Mauriac has at long last written what could be considered to be the very first chapter of the book otherwise already completed fifteen years before.[3]

[1] As in all his novels written after 1936 the natural world plays little part in the total impact of this book. The critical moment when Alain announces his engagement to Marie occurs at the height of summer, but otherwise the seasonal pattern used so effectively in NV or AN is quite absent.

[2] AA, p. 232.

[3] This impression is made particularly real by Mauriac's providing the novel with an open ending.

SELECT BIBLIOGRAPHY

SINCE the publication of Professor Keith Goesch's *François Mauriac. Essai de bibliographie chronologique, 1908–1960* (Nizet, Paris, 1965), the need to append an extensive bibliography to any study of Mauriac's work has been greatly reduced. I have therefore only included details of the *Œuvres complètes* and of those books which have been published since 1956. Where I have consulted other editions details are to be found in the list of abbreviations on pp. x, xi. I have similarly listed only those critical works (books and articles) which I have found particularly relevant for this study.

1. *Works by Mauriac*

Œuvres complètes de François Mauriac, Grasset chez Arthème Fayard, Paris, 12 Volumes, 1956–61.

Le Fils de l'homme, Grasset, Paris, 1958.

Bloc-notes, 1952–1957, Flammarion, Paris, 1958.

Mémoires intérieurs, Flammarion, Paris 1959.

Le Nouveau Bloc-notes, 1958–1960, Flammarion, Paris, 1961.

Ce que je crois, Grasset, Paris, 1962.

De Gaulle, Grasset, Paris, 1964.

Nouveaux Mémoires intérieurs, Flammarion, Paris, 1965.

D'autres et moi, textes recueillis et commentés par Keith Goesch, Grasset, Paris, 1966.

Mémoires politiques, Grasset, Paris, 1967.

Le Nouveau Bloc-notes, 1961–1964, Flammarion, Paris, 1968.

Un Adolescent d'autrefois, Flammarion, Paris, 1969.

2. *Studies of Mauriac's work*

(a) *Books*

BENDZ, ERNST, *François Mauriac, Ebauche d'une figure*, Messageries du livre, Paris, 1946.

CORMEAU, NELLY, *L'Art de François Mauriac*, Grasset, Paris, 1951.

DU BOS, CHARLES, *François Mauriac et le problème du romancier catholique*, Corrêa, Paris, 1933.

SELECT BIBLIOGRAPHY 117

SELECT BIBLIOGRAPHY 117

SELECT BIBLIOGRAPHY 117

FILLON, AMÉLIE, François Mauriac, Edgar Malfère, Paris, 1936.

FLOWER, JOHN, *A critical commentary on Mauriac's 'Le Nœud de vipères'*, Macmillan, London, 1969.

—— *'Les Anges noirs' de François Mauriac. Une étude critique*, Archives des Lettres Modernes, Minard, Paris, 1969.

HOURDIN, GEORGES, *Mauriac, romancier chrétien*, Editions du temps présent, Paris, 1945.

JARETT-KERR, MARTIN, *François Mauriac*, Bowes and Bowes, Cambridge, 1954.

JENKINS, CECIL, *Mauriac*, Oliver and Boyd, Edinburgh and London, 1965.

MAJAULT, JOSEPH, *Mauriac et l'art du roman*, Laffont, Paris, 1946.

MOLONEY, MICHAEL, *François Mauriac, a critical study*, A. Swallow, Denver, 1958.

NORTH, ROBERT, *Le Catholicisme dans l'œuvre de François Mauriac*, Conquistador, Paris, 1950.

PALANTE, ALAIN, *Mauriac, le roman et la vie*, Le Portulan, Paris, 1946.

RIDEAU, EMILE, *Comment lire François Mauriac*, Aux étudiants de France, Paris, 1945.

ROBICHON, JACQUES, *François Mauriac*, Editions universitaires, Paris, 1953.

SIMON, PIERRE-HENRI, *Mauriac par lui-même*, Seuil, Paris, 1953.

STRATFORD, PHILIP, *Faith and Fiction, creative process in Greene and Mauriac*, University of Notre Dame Press, Indiana, 1963.

VANDROMME, POL, *La Politique littéraire de François Mauriac*, Etheel, Paris, 1957.

VIER, JACQUES, *François Mauriac, romancier catholique?* Imprimerie Tancrède, Paris, 1938.

The following more general studies contain useful sections or chapters on Mauriac:

CHAPSAL, MADELEINE, *Les Ecrivains en personne*, Julliard, Paris, 1960.

CURTIS, JEAN-LOUIS, *Haute école*, Julliard, Paris, 1950.

O'BRIEN, CONOR CRUISE [O'DONNELL, DONAT], *Maria Cross*, Chatto and Windus, London 1954.

TURNELL, MARTIN, *The Art of French Fiction*, Hamish Hamilton, London, 1959.

(b) *Articles*

BOERBACH, B.-M. 'Introduction à une étude psychologique et

philosophique de l'œuvre de François Mauriac, *Neophilologus,* 1942, pp. 241–75.

BOERBACH, B.-M., 'La place de la métaphysique dans l'art de M. François Mauriac', *Neophilologus,* 1946, pp. 151–63.

FLOWER, JOHN, 'François Mauriac and Social Catholicism. An episode in *L'Enfant chargé de chaînes*', *French Studies,* April, 1967, pp. 125–38.

HOLDHEIM, WILLIAM, 'Mauriac and Sartre's Mauriac Criticism', *Symposium,* Winter 1962, pp. 245–58.

LABBÉ, JEAN, 'Choix de lettres de Francis Jammes à François Mauriac', *La Table ronde,* February, 1956, pp. 86–108.

LEFÈVRE FRÉDÉRIC, 'Une heure avec François Mauriac', *Nouvelles littéraires,* 23 February 1935.

LE HIR, YVES, 'Temps et durée dans "Le Nœud de vipères" de Mauriac', *Les Lettres romanes,* February 1960, pp. 3–13.

MEIN, MARGARET, 'François Mauriac and Jansenism', *The Modern Language Review,* October 1963, pp. 516–23.

SARTRE, JEAN-PAUL, 'François Mauriac et la liberté', *Situations* I, Gallimard, Paris, 1947, pp. 36–57.

SONNENFELD, ALBERT, 'The Catholic Novelist and the Supernatural', *French Studies,* October 1968, pp. 307–19.

(c) *Editions*

Le Drôle, ed. I. H. Clarke, Harrap, London, 1955.

Le Nœud de vipères, ed. S. T. Stoker and R. Silhol, Harrap, London, 1959.

Le Feu sur la terre, ed. R. J. North, Harrap, London, 1962.

Le Mystère Frontenac, ed. A. M. C. Wilcox, Harrap, London, 1964.

Thérèse Desqueyroux, ed. C. Jenkins, University of London Press, London, 1964.

Le Désert de l'amour, ed. W. Fowlie, Blaisdell Publishing Company, Waltham, Massachusetts, 1968.

3. *Other works consulted*

Listed here are only those books and articles which have been found particularly useful. Details of others are given in the footnotes.

BEAU DE LOMÉNIE, EMMANUEL, *Les Responsabilités des dynasties bourgeoises,* 4 volumes, Denoël, Paris, 1947–63.

BÉGUIN, ALBERT, *Bernanos par lui-même,* Seuil, Paris 1964.

BERL, EMMANUEL, *Mort de la pensée bourgeoise,* Grasset, Paris, 1929.

—— *Mort de la morale bourgeoise,* Gallimard, Paris, 1930.

BERNANOS, GEORGES, *Le Crépuscule des vieux*, Gallimard, Paris, 1956.

BOISDEFFRE, PIERRE DE, *Barrès parmi nous*, Le livre contemporain, Paris, 1952.

CARON, JEANNE, *Le Sillon et la démocratic chrétienne 1894–1910*, Plon, Paris, 1967.

CARTER, A. E., *The Idea of Decadence in French Literature*, 1830–1900, University of Toronto Press, Toronto, 1958.

CHASTENET, JACQUES, *Les grandes heures de la Guyenue*, Colbert, Paris, 1946.

—— *La Belle Epoque*, Fayard, Paris, 1949.

CLAUDEL, PAUL and GIDE, ANDRÉ, *Correspondance*, 1899–1926, Gallimard, Paris, 1949 and JAMMES, FRANCIS and FRIZEAU, GABRIEL, *Correspondance*, 1897–1938, Gallimard, Paris, 1952.

COUSIN, LOUIS, *Vie et doctrine du Sillon*, Emmanuel Vitte, Paris, 1906.

CRUICKSHANK, JOHN (ed.), *The Novelist as Philosopher*, Oxford University Press, London, 1962.

DANSETTE, ADRIEN, *Histoire religieuse de la France contemporaine*, Flammarion, Paris, 1951.

—— *Destin du catholicisme français*, Flammarion, Paris, 1957.

DOMENACH, JEAN-MARIE, *Barrès par lui-même*, Seuil, Paris, 1954.

DU BOS, CHARLES, *What is literature?* Sheed and Ward, London, 1940.

ESTEVE, MICHEL, *Bernanos*, Gallimard, Paris, 1965.

FABRÈGUES, JEAN DE, *Le Sillon de Marc Sangnier*, Perrin, Paris, 1964.

FLOWER, JOHN, 'Forerunners of the Worker-Priests', *Journal of Contemporary History*, Winter 1967, pp. 183–99.

GRIFFITHS, RICHARD, *The Reactionary Revolution*, Constable, London, 1966.

LATREILLE, ANDRÉ and RÉMOND, RENÉ, *Histoire du catholicisme en France*, Vol. III, Spes, Paris, 1962.

MARITAIN, JACQUES, *Art et Scolastique*, Art Catholique, Paris, 1920.

—— *Trois Réformateurs*, Plon, Paris, 1925.

—— *Religion et Culture*, Desclée de Brower, Paris, 1930.

—— *The Responsibility of the Artist*, Charles Scribner, New York, 1960.

MASSI, HENRI, *La pensée de Maurice Barrès*, Mercure de France, Paris, 1909.

MAURANGE, DENISE, *Histoire de Bordeaux*, Editions de l'Ecole Moderne, Cannes, 1956.

MOELLER, JACQUES, *Littérature du XXe siècle et christianisme*, Casterman, Tournai, 1957–61.

RIVIÈRE, JACQUES, *Etudes*, Gallimard, Paris, 1925.

—— *Moralisme et littérature*, Corrêa, Paris, 1932.

RIVIÈRE, JACQUES, *Nouvelles Etudes*, Gallimard, Paris, 1947.

ROLLET, HENRI, *L'Action sociale des catholiques en France*, 1871–1914, Desclée de Brouwer, Paris, 1958.

SAINT-JEAN, ROBERT DE, *Julien Green par lui-même*, Seuil, Paris, 1967.

SANGNIER, MARC, *Le 'plus grand Sillon'*, Au Sillon, Paris, 1907.

—— *Le Sillon, esprit et méthodes*, Au Sillon, Paris, 1905.

WEBER, EUGEN, *Action Française*, Stanford University Press, Stanford, 1962.

INDEX